Further Advance Praise

Since 1989, I have worked with a community based, grassroots, minority led, non-profit organization whose mission is dedicated to improving the poverty life conditions of people in rural areas through support services and education. The association is committed to the development and self-actualization of individuals in need through grassroots efforts at the community level sponsored by public and private partnerships with full participation by local citizens. Pastor Grier has been a great help to me in making sure support services and education are available to the people that are in dire need. He has assisted with resumes and job application completion, and he's trained individuals in how to complete a successful job interview. It is God's will to remove impediments for people so that they can contribute to the Kingdom and be productive. Pastor Grier's work represents the Kingdom well. I am convinced without a doubt that if an individual wants to achieve financial freedom, all they have to do is follow the instructions of his spiritual roadmap. I highly recommend Making Money God's Way for people who want to start or grow a Kingdom business.

— **Minister Emma F. Sinkfield, ICPS**
Executive Director, Family Connection of Warren County, Inc.

Making Money God's Way is rich with biblical principles, wisdom, and insight from personal experience. It's a rare read that can enlighten, instruct, redirect, and encourage in every chapter. Winston, I am thankful for your friendship and passion to share your life with others. Present and future businessmen and women can glean from reading this book and walk away with more understanding of how to win!

— **Quamid Green**
Christian Rapper

My father was Pastor Lawrence Otis Bacon. Winston Grier was like a second son to my father, and he is like a brother to me. As a Pastor, my dad was a spiritual father to Winston. My dad poured a lot of himself into Winston's ministry of the Lord's Word. I know he saw a lot in Winston.

We had a saying in the Army, use the 6 Ps. The six Ps are: Prior Planning Prevents Piss Poor Performance. Pastor Grier has done a masterful job in documenting his journey, and he has united natural and spiritual wisdom in writing this book.

I am proud of Pastor Winston Grier for sharing his wisdom in *Making Money God's Way*, and I know that my dad would be proud of him as well.

— **Pastor Cedric Bacon**

Pastor at Wilkes Memorial C.O.G.I.C.; Chairman of the Tennille District; Asst Chief Adjutant for the Southern Georgia Second Ecclesiastical Jurisdiction for C.O.G.I.C.

Making Money God's Way by Pastor Winston Grier is well written and knowledgeable. I have seen this young man, my nephew, be restored from being a prodigal son to a great pastor and businessman. I am so proud that he has shared his life's experiences. I am sure it will help someone in their struggle with money management. I am proud that I had a hand in helping him to be reared to do what is right. His ministering in scripture and instruction in this book will be a wonderful guide. May God continue to lead and guide him always.

— **Reverend Mary B. Grier**

Pastor, Crawfordville House of God Church, Inc.

I'm a cashier at Loves Truck Stop, and Pastor Winston Grier came in to cash his Comcheck. I was having a very busy evening and accidentally gave him $280 too much without knowing it. Pastor Winston Grier went to his truck and noticed I gave him too much and came back in and returned the $280. I was so grateful because Winston saved me and my job. There was no way I would have been able to explain to my manager how my drawer came up short $280. I know *Making Money God's Way* will be a great book coming from a man of integrity.

— **Sharon Freels**

Testimonials for Pastor Winston Grier

I called and just like the message said they called right back. THE CUSTOMER SERVICE GIVING WAS awesome and very GENUINE. Mr. Grier was very prompt with my order and even followed up before and after my appointment!!!! Highly recommended!
— Bianca Whimper

A&L came to my rescue! I had a tire blow or on I20 @ exit 165 towards Augusta & this very polite, honest, hardworking young man got us back on the road! If I could add photos I so would! I love you guys y'all are the best!
— Kristen Adams

Outstanding customer service, great work. Winston, The Man!!!
— Jorge Hurtado

A&L provides professional service and treats all customers with a high level of respect.
— Antonio Hill

A&L Tire is a blessing from the Lord. I was stuck with a flat tire on the Hwy. All of a sudden this truck pulled up behind me. A very nice gentleman stepped out of his truck with this huge smiled to help me. I can't express how grateful I am for A&L Tire being in the right place at the right time and being watchful. A&L Tire is very dependable, friendly and efficient!! AWESOME SERVICES
— Tangelia Townsend

I am always very well pleased with the service I receive each time I take one of my vehicles to A&L! Winston and his staff go above and beyond to take good care of my vehicles and in a very prompt manner! Not to mention Winston is always very nice and respectable with each encounter! I would highly recommend A&L to anyone to take care of your tired services or auto mechanic needs!!!
— Shatega Evans

The bomb dot com all the way around. Service, price, quality, and courtesy.
— Greg Derry

Very respectful. They'll take care of you. I wouldn't choose or trust anyone else but A&L Tire Center. Keep up the good work. God has really blessed you all.
— Velvet Clemons

Blew two tires on I-20 outside Thompson and called in. I had one spare but had to have at least one tire. The owner came out to the interstate, brought a tire, inspected both my rims and found them bent. Didn't matter for the spare, but meant the tire he brought wouldn't hold right. He could've told me to kick rocks and go buy some new rims, but instead he sledgehammered my rim back straight enough to where it would hold to get me the next few hours home and did it all on the side of the interstate in the rain. Also used his gun to tighten down my spare, which he didn't have to do. Very much appreciated and glad I busted my tires near them.
— Zachary Faircloth

Me and my family of 6 were stuck over the 4th of July weekend with no spare, no luck of a successful tow, nor Uber. After 5 hours of being sitting ducks on I20, their service got us a tire in the middle of the morning of 4th of July! Words cannot express the gratitude we have for your business!!! God bless you and we are forever grateful!!!
— LaShay Harvey

Absolutely the best customer service anywhere. Fixed the rim and changed the tire. When they tell you don't worry, that they'll get you back on the road, they mean it.
— Jerry Walker

I purchased this scooter from A&L Tire Center. Great customer service. Worked hard to get me what I wanted. If you're looking for ATVs, scooters, golf carts etc, give them a call. You won't regret it, it's an easy process!!!
— Eric Fuller

I am from out of town and had a flat on a rainy Friday evening. They came within 20 minutes of calling them. I was super impressed with the professional service. I was definitely thankful for their hard work and gracious help
— Karen Phillips

I had the best experience I could have hoped for. They had the tires I needed, and threw in an extra at no charge. The price was quite reasonable, and they brought them to me. The guys I talked to were both friendly, helpful and professional. I look forward to doing business with them again
— Sandra Blount

Pastor Grier's Guide To
Building A Kingdom Business

MAKING MONEY GOD'S WAY

WINSTON GRIER

First Edition

Editing Services by Caitlin Freeman of Get Bookified
Book Cover, Typesetting and Layout Design Copyright © 2022
Maja Creative
Art Direction by Maja Wolnik of Maja Creative
Graphic Design by Monika Brzeczek of Maja Creative

ISBN PRINT: 979-8-9867503-1-6
ISBN EBOOK: 979-8-9867503-0-9

Published by Winston Grier
www.wealthandkingdom.com

Dedication and Thanks

This book is dedicated to my mom, the late First Lady Betty Jean Howard Grier

In 1988, when I was twelve years old, my mom died and left me with a large inheritance. I'm glad she thought so highly of me to name me the beneficiary of this inheritance. It has gotten me a long way in my business. My mom didn't leave me with a large amount of money; however, before she left, she taught me the importance of prayer, doing things God's way, showing love to people, having a good work ethic, and being obedient to God's Word.

What my mom left me was worth more than all the riches of this world. My mom was the best business owner I knew. She sold her own cooking for years out of her station wagon to help my dad provide for us. Then she opened her restaurant.

When I was a child, my mom showed me what operating a business is all about. One of the things I observed from her was that when you invest in a business, make sure it's something you're passionate about. Cooking and baking was my mom's gift, and she loved it. According to scripture, your gift should open doors for you. She was a great chef, a talented people-person, and she enjoyed serving others.

Back in the 80s when my mom was in business, she would shop around for the best price on food. She kept coupons and sale papers so she could save money to keep her prices affordable. Mom could tell anyone what grocery store had the best price on certain meats or who had the best quality of meat. In those days money was very limited; however, my mom made the best of it. Five days a week, my mom would get up early for work, get on her knees, and pray that God would order her steps and prosper her business.

In those days Walmart didn't make birthday cakes, so people would always call my mother to bake cakes. When churches had special occasions, they would often hire her to do cakes and pies. My mom lived according to God's plan, and God's way. Indeed,

I've never seen the righteous forsaken. My mom would always prepare and plan in advance, so she didn't encounter setbacks.

In the mid-mornings, shortly after seeking God through prayer and cooking, my mom would gather us, and we would start loading the car with food that my mom had prepared. We stayed in a small town called Mayfield GA. It had only one store in the entire city, which was owned by my mom's brother. There were no factories in Mayfield, so we had to drive twenty miles away to Warrenton GA and go to two large factories, Jebco & Georgia Pacific. We would sell food in the parking lot to the employees while they were on their lunch break. My mom's prices and food were so good that it was better for the employees to purchase from her and not leave the job site. The majority of the time, she would give the last few plates away to those who didn't have enough money to purchase.

Later, as her business grew, she opened a restaurant near our church in Thomson GA, selling soul food directly across from a factory. This plant was called National Home Company. They had three departments that took lunch at different times, and she fed at least 75% of their staff. Her restaurant was packed every day, and money was never an issue.

In my young life, I witnessed my mom's passion to perfect her skill, and I saw her commitment to her customers. I watched her grow her business from selling plates from the back of her station wagon to having industry workers coming daily to her restaurant.

My mom was a woman with a loving heart and compassion, and she treated her employees with the utmost respect. She loved her business, she was dedicated to her family, and most of all, she stayed true to the Kingdom while pursuing her financial goals. She had monthly religious days, and she would never open her restaurant on those days, regardless of how much money she could make. When things were tough, mom trusted God to always fulfill her needs. Because of her obedience to God's words, God always provided for her.

My mom has always been a big inspiration to me as a business owner. The Lord was always first in her life, and she allowed nothing to get between her and God's way, not even money.

She taught me great business skills as a child, and she exemplified Making Money God's Way! You are missed, mom, but never forgotten.

Rest in Peace, Mom. Thank You.

Special Thanks to my dad, Apostle Winston Grier, Sr., and my terrific stepmom, First Lady Grier

My dad has always been a devoted father. What impresses me the most about my dad is that when my mom died at the age of forty, he was left with five children, and he raised us all with no complaints. My dad later remarried, and God blessed me with the best stepmom to help my dad out.

I was raised as a PK (preacher's kid) by a great spiritual leader in my dad who always honored God's words with his actions. My dad has always taught me scripture, and all of my biblical wisdom has come from his teaching, leading, and training. Unfortunately, as a teenager, I was rebellious and hardheaded. As a young man, I left my father's house and turned to the streets. Despite my errant ways, my dad would always pray over me that God would restore my mind back to Kingdom principles.

I returned back to God in my thirties with God's grace. Thanks to my dad's intercessory prayers, I was saved from the enemy. I always wanted my own business, and later I left my job and started my own business making money God's Way. My dad has always given me great financial advice. I will never forget it, he came to me one day and said, "Here is a great lesson, son. I know we don't need money in heaven, but here on earth, you don't have to go broke." In other words, there is nothing wrong with living for God while pursuing financial freedom. I will be forever grateful for my dad, who never gave up on his prodigal son.

Special Thanks to my wife, Krystal Denyel Grier

My wife, Krystal Grier, has been a tremendous support to my business through the good and bad times. She has held down the house for a long time when I was running 24/7, trying to get my business off the ground. Krystal was always there with our kids when I couldn't show up for games, honor days, etc.

The word of God is true when He says, find a wife, find a good thing. I will admit, my wife is indeed my good thing. Without her, there would be no me. My wife has been patient while I made mistakes as a business owner, sometimes even jeopardizing our finances and harming my family. Even in times when no one believed in me, my wife did. She has given me confidence to keep pushing when I wanted to throw in the towel. She stood beside me when I didn't have a penny, loving me unconditionally. I'm grateful for her, her love, her support, and her patience in my darkest hours.

Krystal, Thank You, and I love you for always being you!!

TABLE OF CONTENTS

Introduction

At the time of this writing (August 2022), I've been a minister for nine years, a Pastor for six years, and over the past fifteen years, I've owned several businesses. I started out in business before I had a serious relationship with God, and so I've seen the ups and downs of doing business, both in a worldly way and in accordance with God. Some of my businesses have succeeded, and some have failed, but what I know is that every business has done better when I make money God's Way.

It is disheartening to me to see Kingdom people who love God be filled with a spiritual anointing and yet live in a state of lack. I have seen some business owners declare bankruptcy, not understanding why they can't succeed. I know where they're coming from. There was a time when I defined myself as a business owner who failed, and I was totally at a loss as to why.

Making money is not reserved for people of the world. God's people should not have to look on, starving, while worldly people live in financial overflow. Financial abundance is our inheritance as Kingdom people. I believe we should be good examples of God in every area of our life, and we must not exclude financial success from that list. Yes, we can quote Scripture, pray in tongues, and preach the Gospels, but if our bank account is at 0, we will not be effective at spreading God's Word.

Whether we want to believe it or not, those with money have authority and power. Few listen to people who are broke. From my years reading the Bible, I know that Abraham, Solomon, David, and even Job lived in abundance of possessions. They were wealthy men, but they acquired their wealth in accordance with God's Way, and God rewarded them for that. The Bible says that Job was the greatest man on the East side of the world, and after his trials, God rewarded him with tremendous prosperity. So, if the men in the Bible were living great, why aren't we?

In my book, my goal is to teach you how to Make Money God's Way. My goal is to also share with you why God's Way matters. Making money should never take the place of living righteously; it must never interfere with your marriage or cause you to neglect your family. All these things are important to God.

We must walk in the things God has promised us, and prosperity is one of those things. I believe God when He says you shall be a lender and not a borrower. We should be the head and not the tail. I don't believe the world and those who don't live obedient to God's Way are supposed to have all the riches of the world while we live in financial strain.

We serve God when we preach a good sermon, pray a nice prayer, and tell a good testimony, but we cannot build the Kingdom if we are always robbing Peter to pay Paul.

In this book, I share my successes and failures in business to illuminate the path that God has shown me. My words are backed by scriptures from God because the Lord always has the final say. If God said it, you can believe it. If you take heed to God's word, you will walk in overflow, see God's favor over your life, and your business and financial increase will be inevitable.

Yes, you may fail sometimes, but if you make God the Lord of your life and live according to Him, He will reward you mentally, physically, spiritually, and financially. The lessons in my book take time, hard work, and diligence. You will find no "get rich quick" lessons here; I firmly believe that there is no way to become a millionaire overnight. My book offers a method of slow and steady improvement, so that you can achieve true financial success over time.

I believe in my heart that if we're not experiencing the financial overflow that God has promised, then we're not doing what the Bible has instructed us to do. As you read the following chapters, you will find out the mistakes I made that kept me from prospering. Reading how I failed and learning how to get it right will be a blessing to you, your children, and your children's children.

Dear reader, I offer you this prayer

Oh most gracious, kind, faithful, and heavenly Father. I pray now that You would reach out to whoever is reading this book and open their eyes to see every valuable insight that you have given me. Oh Lord, bless the person holding this book and allow them to achieve prosperity.

Father, You have said in Your words that we have not because we ask not. I humble myself now, asking You to order this reader's steps. Please lead and guide them so they may live in financial overflow, and more importantly, bring Glory to Your name. Dear Lord, as a servant of God, I come now interceding for this reader that whatever has them in captivity, You would break the hands of the enemy over their life.

Father, we know Satan comes to steal, kill, and destroy, but You have come that we may live an abundant life. We bind any spirit of lack, any financial bondage, and we loose Your abundant blessing. Lord, we realize we can do nothing without You, so I pray that You would protect this reader's name from any Satanic schemes from their enemies that are sent to destroy this person's life or business endeavors. Lord, I trust You to connect this reader to the right mentor, right supplier, right employees, and right customers, and I ask that You bring them financial increase and Kingdom connections that will be pleasing in Your sight. All these blessings I ask for in Your son Jesus' name. Amen.

1

**COMMIT YOUR WORK
TO THE LORD, AND
YOUR PLANS WILL
SUCCEED**

CHAPTER 1

Commit Your Work to the Lord, and Your Plans Will Succeed

When I first started my business, I had a good idea and a wish list. At the age of thirty, I quit my job and opened a used tire store in my city of Thomson, Georgia. I sold my vehicle and purchased a service truck so that I could start a roadside division. This roadside division was an extension of standard towing and on-the-spot mobile tire service. My team would drive out to assist individuals within a twenty-mile radius who had gotten a flat tire on the side of the road and couldn't make it to my shop.

At the time I opened my business, I was the only used tire shop in my city. I purchased my equipment from a man who was getting ready to quit the tire business. When I bought him out, he was finally able to retire. I was confident that

I could sell plenty of tires in the store, but I was even more confident that I could build a successful roadside team, something the previous owner had never been able to do. I was certain that drivers who'd suffered a blowout would pay top dollar for my roadside crew to install new tires. I was so sure of this, in fact, that I didn't do any research to see whether customers in my area wanted and would pay for this service. I was caught up in the dream of quick financial gain, and let's just say that I failed miserably.

I was ignorant about running a tire business, and my haste to make money blinded me to my inexperience. I thought to myself, "Everybody needs tires, right? So, why shouldn't I be the one that they go to when they need their old tires replaced?" It seemed like a failsafe way to earn a living. Alas, I didn't get any of the results I wanted. I worked countless hours and sleepless nights, trying to get my business off the ground, but I still wasn't seeing any financial growth. I was always robbing Peter to pay Paul. Some Fridays I would pay my bills and my employees, but I didn't have enough money to pay myself. This happened to me for many years. After all, I hadn't educated myself about the tire industry, so how could I expect to win?

I share this story to illustrate one of the biggest unnecessary costs in business, and that is the cost of poor planning.

I started my business with a wish and a prayer, but no solid business plan. I didn't think I needed to do any research. Since I owned the only used tire business in my city, it just seemed like a no-brainer that stranded motorists would call my shop for roadside assistance. However, if I had done a thorough analysis beforehand, I would

JOHN 10:27
My sheep hear My voice; I know
them, and they follow Me.

PSALMS 37:23
The LORD directs the steps of
the Kingdom, He delights in
every area of our lives.

JOSHUA 1:8
This Book of the Law shall not depart from
your mouth, but you shall meditate in it
day and night, that you may observe to
do according to all that is written in it. For
then you will make your way prosperous,
and then you will have good success.

have learned that the majority of motorists pay for a roadside assistance plan, like AAA. When they are stranded on the side of the road with a flat tire, they call their roadside assistance company. The company then sends a tow truck to bring their vehicle to an affiliated tire shop, where the driver can get tires installed for a lower price than they would pay out of pocket for a business like mine to send a road crew out to them.

At first, I thought that there was something I was doing wrong that was causing motorists to avoid my business, but I slowly came to realize that the problem was due to the simplest of economic principles: costs and benefits. Motorists are un-likely to call a local company to perform a service that they are already paying for, even if the local company performs a superior service.

I share this story to illustrate one of the biggest unnecessary costs in business, and that is the cost of poor planning. Due to my poor planning, I didn't know in advance that most drivers have easy access to a roadside assistance plan through their auto insurance or cell phone company. What I had believed to be a lucrative business idea had turned out to be a colossal waste of time and money. I had no one to blame for my poor planning but myself.

My goal as you read my book is to show you how to prosper in business by staying true to your Kingdom responsibilities. I hate seeing people fail, and I'm so thrilled to teach you how to be financially successful, how to avoid pitfalls, and most of all, how to make money by doing things God's Way.

I learned from these early mistakes, and I now partner with AAA, GEICO, and State Farm, among other companies. They send business to me, and I provide roadside tire services to their customers. This marketing strategy was one of the many important lessons that I learned from running my business: customer acquisition is costly, so whenever possible, partner with a company that will bring customers to you.

In Hosea 4:6, the scripture tells us: "People are destroyed for lack of knowledge." I didn't know any better, and so I didn't invest my money wisely. My lack of knowledge cost me years of my life and hundreds of thousands of dollars. I hadn't studied the tire industry or weighed the pros and cons, but somehow in my ignorance I thought I had it all figured out.

I might have been uneducated about business, but I knew God. My father is a preacher, and I grew up in the Church. I have always had a strong faith in God, which ultimately led me to becoming a Pastor. In my struggles, I turned to God for help. I started reading the scripture to look for what it says about earning money. Through my studies, I realized that all the business knowledge we need is contained in the Bible. The scripture tells us how to be successful in business by making money God's Way.

Doing Business God's Way

First of all, let me be very clear — God doesn't want us to be reckless with our money; He doesn't want us investing our hard-earned dollars on a business that's based solely on our wishes and hopes for prosperity. We must be careful how we invest our resources.

God wants us to make wise investments. He tells us that this is His will in the Parable of the Talents in Matthew 25:14–30:

For the Kingdom of Heaven is like a man traveling to a far country, who called his servants and entrusted his wealth to them. To one servant he gave five talents, to another two, and to another one, to each according to his own ability. Then he went on a journey. The servant who had received the five talents went and traded with them, and he made another five talents. And likewise, he who had received two gained two more also. But he who had received one went and dug in the ground, and there he hid his lord's money. After a long time, the lord of those servants returned and settled accounts with them.

So he who had received five talents came and brought five other talents, saying, "Lord, you delivered to me five talents; look, I have gained five more talents besides them." His lord said to him, "Well done, good and faithful servant; you were faithful over a few things, I will make you ruler over many things. Enter into the joy of your lord."

He also who had received two talents came and said, "Lord, you delivered to me two talents; look, I have gained two more talents besides them." His lord said to him, "Well done, good and faithful servant; you have been faithful over a few things, I will make you ruler over many things. Enter into the joy of your lord."

Then he who had received the one talent came and said, "Lord, I knew you to be a hard man, reaping where you have not sown, and gathering where you have not scattered seed. And I was afraid, and went and hid your talent in the ground. Look, there you have what is yours."

HOSEA 4:6

My people are destroyed for lack of knowledge.

PROVERBS 19:2

Desire without knowledge is not good, and whoever makes haste with his feet misses his way.

But his lord answered and said to him, "You wicked and lazy servant, you knew that I reap where I have not sown, and gather where I have not scattered seed. So you ought to have deposited my money with the bankers, and at my coming I would have received back my own with interest. So take the talent from him, and give it to him who has ten talents. For to everyone who has, more will be given, and he will have abundance; but from him who does not have, even what he has will be taken away. And cast the unprofitable servant into the outer darkness. In that place there will be weeping and gnashing of teeth."

When I read the Parable of the Talents, I see three main lessons for entrepreneurs and business owners. The first lesson is that God rewards us when we make wise investments that gain a profit. The second lesson is that God doesn't want us sitting around looking up at the sky, waiting for Him to shower us with money while we put in little to no effort. The third, and most important lesson, is that God gives each of us an opportunity to make money on our investments; however, if we don't make intelligent financial decisions, He will take what we have earned and give it to someone else.

I don't want you to lose years in business the way I did, so my ultimate goal is to teach you how to prosper in business and in your personal life. In this book, I share my successes and failures in order to help you run a sustainable and profitable business. If you want to start a business, don't do what I did in the beginning, or you will accumulate unnecessary business debt. This ignorant approach leads to many setbacks; indeed, it caused me to push my retirement to a much later time in my life than I had planned. It nearly destroyed me and my business on many occasions, and it threatened to dismantle my family.

I've heard so many people say that experience is the best teacher, and I agree with this in certain contexts. In business, however, learning from experience often comes at too high a cost. Learning from experience eventually caused me to file bankruptcy. Because of this bankruptcy, I was no longer able to purchase my inventory with credit, and all of my purchases had to be paid out of pocket. If you're an existing business owner, then you know how hard it is to operate out of your account due to bad credit. I share this story with you as a cautionary tale, and I urge you to protect your credit because having bad credit will cripple your business, especially when you are starting out.

New entrepreneurs simply can't afford the amount of trial and error that it takes to build a business from scratch. I don't want you to lose tens of thousands of dollars learning from experience because sometimes you never recover from those lessons. Instead, I share my advice so you can avoid the pitfalls that I've encountered. Reading this book will allow you to benefit from my mistakes and avoid bringing harm to your business.

Here are some of the lessons that I've learned from my early business mistakes:

- Research the market, your competitors, and your potential business location.
- Find out the population of your city to see if there is enough demand for the product or service that you will supply.
- Know exactly how much it will take to start this business.

MATTHEW 6:33

But seek first the Kingdom of God and His righteousness, and all these things shall be added to you.

2 TIMOTHY 2:19

Nevertheless the solid foundation of God stands, having this seal: "The LORD knows those who are His," and, "Let everyone who names the name of Christ depart from iniquity."

PROVERBS 28:26

He who trusts in his own heart is a fool, but whoever walks wisely will be delivered.

PROVERBS 27:12

The prudent see danger and take refuge, but the simple keep going and pay the penalty.

- Educate yourself and learn about the industry you're looking to invest in.
- Know your product value, the wholesale cost, and connect with numerous suppliers.
- Have four or five different suppliers in the US and/or internationally. Look for suppliers that have a good balance between quality products and low prices. Start with a small order, and then build up trust with the supplier.
- Develop a marketing and advertisement strategy based on the needs of your business and your ideal customer. Even if you have the best products and services in the world, you won't serve the Kingdom if you don't put yourself out there.
- More than anything, know your worth as a business owner — what unique qualities do you bring to the table that your competitors don't possess?
- Seek out formal education to strengthen your business knowledge, with a major caveat — as much as possible, avoid incurring academic debt:
  - If you decide to go to college, seek out scholarships and grants. Student loans will hamstring you and your business for decades to come.
  - Also, look into trade schools and apprenticeships.
  - Read business books about your industry, and study the careers of industry leaders.
  - Get a business mentor or coach who will share their experiences and teach you along the way. That is where I come in!

My goal as you read my book is to show you how to prosper in business by staying true to your Kingdom responsibilities. I hate seeing people fail, and I'm so thrilled to teach you how to be financially successful, how to avoid pitfalls, and most of all, how to make money by doing things God's Way.

The Power of a Kingdom Business Plan

In business, planning is key. Developing a detailed business plan allows you to gather information, study the market, hire a qualified business attorney who knows your industry, meditate on God, and follow the path that God has directed you to take. When you do things God's Way and create a Kingdom plan, you will see your business flourish.

As part of your planning, you must do your due diligence to understand your business' pros and cons, your competitors' strengths and weaknesses, and the number of potential customers in your location. It is important to educate yourself on your industry investment and have evidence that this investment will yield a good return. To be successful in business, you must put in a great deal of work. Laziness will put you out of business fast. Faith without work is useless. When you don't know what to do, or have made some bad business decisions, ask God to open your eyes and preserve your business. When you serve God, He will help you succeed.

In the financial crash of 2008, I saw four or five other tire businesses like mine close their doors. I saw many other businesses close during

JOSHUA 1:7

Be strong and very courageous, that you may observe to do according to all the law which Moses My servant commanded you; do not turn from it to the right hand or to the left, that you may prosper wherever you go.

JOB 36:11-12

If they obey and serve Him, they shall spend their days in prosperity, and their years in pleasures. But if they do not obey, they shall perish, and they shall die without knowledge.

1 CHRONICLES 4:10

And Jabez called on the God of Israel saying, "Oh, that You would bless me indeed, and enlarge my territory, that Your hand would be with me, and that You would keep me from evil, that I may not cause pain!" So God granted him what he requested.

the Covid-19 pandemic, but God kept me going. I'm still here, not because I'm a business genius — I'm here because I serve God, and when you serve God, it pays off. When you serve God, you are partnering with Him. He wants to see you succeed because that's what a good business partner does. Why? Because when you succeed, the Kingdom succeeds. Satan doesn't want Kingdom people to prosper. He wants us to give up and throw in the towel. That's why I share my story. Even when you lack knowledge, God is going to step in for you if you partner with Him. He will help you win in ways that you can't even foresee.

> **In my struggles, I turned to God for help. I started reading the scripture to look for what it says about earning money. Through my studies, I realized that all the business knowledge we need is contained in the Bible.**

Map Out Your Kingdom Business Plan

We listen to God, not only for personal guidance, but also for our direction in business. And yet, we won't succeed if we wait for God to carry us. We have to put in the work, placing one foot in front of the other as we move forward along our path.

Benjamin Franklin once said, "If you fail to plan, you are planning to fail." Franklin was simply saying that success doesn't happen by accident; we won't prosper by playing the lottery with our business every week and hoping we get lucky. If you want to achieve prosperity, you must put in the work.

PROVERBS 16:3

Commit your works unto the LORD, and He will establish your plans.

PROVERBS 14:12

There is a way that seems right to a man, but its end is the way of death.

PSALM 119:105

Your word is a lamp unto my feet, and a light unto my path.

Write out your Kingdom business plan so you know where your business is going and what it will take to get there:

1. **Write down your vision for your business.** Place this vision within your heart and your mind. When you record your vision, make sure that it is based on your Kingdom responsibilities. Create a list of specific goals that you want your business to accomplish. For example:

    i. I want my business to support my family.

    ii. I want my business to make it possible for me to tithe more than 10%.

    iii. I want my business to allow me to represent the Kingdom within my community.

    iv. I want my business to allow me to utilize my God-given gifts.

2. **Write down your plan for your business.** Your business plan will require some research on your part. Make it specific, reasonable, and achievable. You can visit the Small Business Administration for sample business plans.[1] The following list will give you a good place to start:

    i. To accomplish my vision above, I need to make a yearly income of:

    ii. My business idea is:

    iii. The specific problems I want my business to solve are:

    iv. My products and/or services are:

    v. The ideal customer I want to serve is:

    vi. My business is brick-and-mortar, online, or both:

---

1 "Write your business plan." U.S. Small Business Administration. www.sba.gov/business-guide/plan-your-business/write-your-business-plan

vii. Based on my business idea and my ideal customer profile, my marketing and advertising plan is (e.g., online advertising, TV or radio ads, local networking within the community, etc.):

viii. My competitors in my local area are:

ix. My competitors online are:

x. Is the market for this business idea saturated? If so, consider pivoting to a different business idea or niching the business idea further:

xi. The unique differentiators that set me apart from my competitors are:

xii. Based on the current market, my product/service price range is:

xiii. Based on the needs of my business, I expect my yearly expenses to be:

xiv. Based on my price range and my expenses, my sales per month need to be $$ in order to make a profit:

xv. Based on all the numbers above, my projected yearly income and expenses are:

3. **Go through the business plan and crunch the numbers** to understand what it will take to be successful.

i. Let God guide you. If the numbers show that this business plan won't be profitable, give God your thanks for this knowledge, and revise your plan.

ii. Don't spend years bootstrapping a business that doesn't work. Pivot when you need to. Starting out right with a solid plan will save you time and money in the long run.

4. **Pray to God and ask Him how He wants your business to serve the Kingdom.**
    i. What are the specific goals that God wants you to achieve with your business?
    ii. What is your business mission, and how does this mission serve the Kingdom?
    iii. What are ways that you can share God's Word to comfort and uplift your customers?
    iv. What are ways that God wants you to give back financially to the Kingdom, so that both your business and the Kingdom can prosper?
5. **Ask God to reveal to you your unique gifts** and talents that you bring to the world. God will make mighty use of you with whatever gifts He has placed in you.
    i. Map out your gifts. Everyone has something they do that adds to the Kingdom in a unique way.
    ii. Ask yourself what you are passionate about. Each area of passion will indicate a gift that God has placed in you.
    iii. Look for ways to bring your unique gifts into your business. In my case, my passion is for sharing the Word of God through public speaking. When I have the opportunity, I bring this gift to my business by sharing the goodness of God with my customers to comfort them in their time of need.

JAMES 2:20

Do you not know that faith without works is useless?

PROVERBS 3:5

Trust in the LORD with all your heart, and lean not on your own understanding; in all your ways acknowledge Him, and He shall direct your paths.

6. **Find a business mentor.** Seek out a Kingdom businessperson who can guide you as you build your business.
    i. Kingdom people work together to help each other out. There's no way for you to know everything when you first start out in business, so wisdom and expert guidance is invaluable.
    ii. I am here to serve you as a Kingdom business mentor and coach. Please reach out to me for guidance. I want to help you so that your business can serve God. When the Kingdom prospers, everyone prospers.
7. **Always seek God and let Him direct you** in your business.
    i. The most important part of your Kingdom business plan is doing what God wants for you. You can build a business plan that looks like it will be successful, but if it is out of alignment with God, it will likely fail.
    ii. Pray to God. He is your partner in your business. Don't just jump up and follow the first business idea that comes to you. Tell Him your plans. Then listen for His answer. Once you've gotten His permission to go forward, follow His plan for you.

Represent God in Your Business

One day a few years ago, I was feeling exhausted from business fatigue. I was disappointed because I knew that 3 John 3:2 says, "Beloved, I pray that you may prosper in all things and be in health, just as your soul prospers." Yet I didn't think I was getting the result I had hoped for from that verse.

I then decided to pray and meditate with God about what I was doing wrong. I asked the Lord, "God, why am I not living in abundance?" God revealed to me that I wasn't including my Kingdom responsibilities in my business, and I was disobedient to several of His commands. God showed me that a true Kingdom businessman should always include God in his business plan.

God gives each of us an opportunity to make money on our investments; however, if we don't make intelligent financial decisions, He will take what we have earned and give it to someone else.

I prayed on this revelation, and I realized that I had never really planned my business with God being my foundation. I humbled myself like Paul in Acts 9:6 and said, "Lord what would you rather me do for you as I pursue my business goals?"

God said to me, "I have been sending you to help stranded motorists day and night — people stuck on the side of the road with flat tires, busted radiators, and blown out motors. These people are having the most difficult times in their life. You have been providing towing and roadside services for over fourteen years, and yet you haven't shared a word with most of these people to draw them closer to Me."

JEREMIAH 29:11

"For I know the thoughts that I think toward you," says the LORD, "thoughts of peace, and not of evil, to give you a future and a hope."

WINSTON GRIER

As a Pastor I was shocked and ashamed to see that I had missed out on so many opportunities to share the goodness of God in my business. I'm not making any excuses for my decisions, but sometimes we don't want to mix God in our business. But that way of thinking is for those who are not on the battlefield for God. As Kingdom men and women, it is our duty to include God. We must remember that our business should exemplify God and be a light to the world. I had been helping customers in distress every day, and yet I had failed to share the goodness of God with them to help them in their difficult times. Everyone we meet in our business gives us the opportunity to share the good news about our Lord and Savior Jesus Christ.

The very next day, I sat down and started creating inspirational cards with verses from scripture that I could give to customers when they bought tires or paid for emergency services. I used my knowledge of the Bible to create messages that I knew would be meaningful and uplifting to my customers. It was a simple way to spread the Word of God and comfort people who were having a bad day.

> **When you serve God, you are partnering with Him. He wants to see you succeed because that's what a good business partner does. Why? Because when you succeed, the Kingdom succeeds.**

I remember one time, I handed an inspirational card to a customer, and tears came to his eyes. He said, "Thank you for this. You know, this card is confirmation for some things I've been dealing with lately. You don't know how much you've helped me just now." He was genuinely moved by the Word of God.

At these challenging times, God wanted me to reassure my customers that their light afflictions

JAMES 1:5

If any of you lacks wisdom, let him ask of God, who gives to all liberally and without reproach, and it will be given to you.

MATTHEW 5:16

Let your light so shine before men, that they may see your good works, and glorify your Father in heaven.

were but for a moment and remind them that He would never leave or forsake them. Once I started to represent God in my business, my customers multiplied, and my business began to prosper.

This was an ordained appointment that the Lord planned for me, and I promised Him that from that day forward, I would include God and Kingdom principles in every interaction.

And so it is that in every moment that benefits your business financially, you must first ask God, "What are my Kingdom responsibilities in this transaction?" Whenever you are given the opportunity, you should take the time to make an impact on someone spiritually. Don't miss those moments to represent the Kingdom.

Kingdom Business Questions

Ask yourself these seven Kingdom business questions to determine the role that God plays in your business now:

- Are you representing God in your business?
- Have you sought God for advice on what direction to take in your business?
- What do you plan to contribute to the Kingdom?
- How will your business accomplish your Kingdom contribution?
- How will helping your ideal customer serve the Kingdom?
- Would your Pastor be proud of your business?
- Are you letting your light shine by running your business?

Pastor Grier's Foundation Prayer for Your Business

Dear kind and heavenly Father. As I bow before You today, I ask that You would order my steps. Lead and guide me in the direction You have for me and my business to take. God, I trust You because You have said in Your words, "I am God, and there is none like Me. I declare the end from the beginning, and ancient times from what is still to come. I say, 'My purpose will stand, and all My good pleasure I will accomplish." (Isaiah 46:9–10) Lord, You are the Foundation, and I know my business won't prosper without Your guidance. Speak, for Your servant hears.

Amen.

2

**WHEN YOU WALK
IN INTEGRITY, YOU
WALK SECURELY**

CHAPTER 2

When You Walk in Integrity, You Walk Securely

Honesty Matters

I will never forget the time I purchased some tires from a man at a deeply discounted price. I didn't know for sure, but I had a gut feeling that those tires were stolen. Still, I pushed aside my misgivings, and I allowed Satan to tempt me. I placed my financial gain over my Christian values. I'm fully aware that the Scriptures say, "Thou shalt not steal," and yet I partook in that sin to save a few dollars.

According to Scripture, "We must obey the laws of the land" (Romans 13:1), and it is a crime to buy something stolen. It is called theft by receiving. Kingdom men and women must not break the law, for breaking the law is going against the Will of God.

Satan had turned my mind from God and made me fixate on the potential profits I could make from the deal. Deep down, I had a feeling that I was doing something wrong. I now know that this feeling was God telling me, "Winston, you know those tires are stolen. Are you really going to buy them?" Despite God's warning, I went ahead with the deal. I bought the tires and I stored them in my shop. Within a matter of days, my service calls slowed and then stopped completely. My service calls were the lifeblood of my tire business, so when they vanished, I knew that I was in trouble.

I paid a price for being disobedient to both God's law and man's law. I didn't get any service calls for three or four months, and I was never able to sell those tires. God made sure that I did not profit from that stolen property. I didn't go to jail, but I still paid a heavy penalty because my business took a big loss. Kingdom men and women must be honest and keep a good reputation. We can't engage in wrongdoing or treat our customers unfairly and think we're going to get away with it. Let me warn you, God will make you pay. I understand now the meaning of Proverbs 14:2, "He who walks in his uprightness fears the Lord, but he who is perverse in his ways despises Him."

> **We must serve as good examples to the world, beginning with having integrity.**

God ensured that I paid my penance for my disobedience. I soon found myself in a position where I needed money to pay business expenses — the bills came rather quickly when the phone calls stopped. I had invested a great deal of money in those stolen tires. I'd planned to sell the tires at their market price, which would mean that I could make a significant profit over what I had spent, but God ensured that this didn't happen. He expected better of me. He wanted me to do business His way.

PROVERBS 22:1

A good name is rather to be chosen than great riches, and loving favor rather than silver and gold.

PSALMS 37:16-17

The little that a righteous man has is better than the riches of many wicked men. For the arms of the wicked shall be broken.

PROVERBS 10:9

He who walks in integrity walks securely, but he who makes his ways crooked will be found out.

ROMANS 12:9

Let love be without pretense. Abhor what is evil. Hold fast to what is good.

Now, even though I had paid 75% less than what I would have paid wholesale, it meant nothing since I had no buyers calling to purchase my inventory. So, I ended up selling the tires to somebody else for even less than what I had paid for them just so I could have some money for past-due bills.

When I tell you that God will make you pay, trust me — He will. I didn't profit anything. After all, how could I expect to flourish when the Scriptures speak against it? Proverbs 14:11 says, "The house of the wicked shall be overthrown, but the tabernacle of the upright shall flourish." I know firsthand the importance of taking your time and doing things the right way. What looked like a good opportunity for me to prosper turned out to be a bad loss. The Scriptures are true: "Wealth gained by dishonesty will soon diminish, but he who gathers by labor will increase." (Proverbs 13:11) I didn't gain anything from purchasing stolen goods; instead, I came close to losing my business.

Financial gain alone doesn't make us good Kingdom businessmen or businesswomen if we're not obedient to God's Word. We must serve as good examples to the world, beginning with having integrity. Let your light shine so other Kingdom people can see that running a business and gaining financial freedom can be done honestly. I'm reminded of why the Bible said, "The little that a righteous man has is better than the riches of the wicked." (Psalm 37:16) Why? Because God holds us to a higher standard; He expects us to operate our business with honor and uprightness. Proverbs 16:2 says, "All the ways of a man are pure in his own eyes, but the Lord tests his integrity." As Kingdom business owners, we will be tested, and we must pass each test or temptation that comes our way. Honesty will cause your sales to increase. It may take a little longer to prosper and grow your business, but it's all worth it in the end. Your reputation depends on your customer's belief and trust in your business, so don't ruin it with deceit. A good reputation can help you get new leads, new contracts, and happy repeat customers. Most importantly, it will allow God to bestow favor on you and open doors for your business that you didn't even foresee. Dishonesty will destroy your name and your reputation; it will paralyze your business or close it altogether.

Bouncing Back with Grace

As a business owner, you may be thinking, "I'm not sure if I would have told the world about that story of purchasing stolen tires." The reason I am happy to share my story is because it can teach other Kingdom business owners three important lessons about doing business God's Way.

- **The first lesson** is that when we try to do things that bring us profit for our business in an ungodly way, God will make us pay for it.
- **The second lesson** is that we must not put limits on God. When we take dishonest routes, we're saying to God, "I don't quite trust you to supply all my business needs."
- **The third lesson** is that when we make bad choices or do something dishonest, we must ask for forgiveness and do right by God.

Above all, you must trust that this is not the end. God is faithful and will allow you to bounce back from your mistakes. Once you know better, do better.

I believe there are times in business where you will have to learn the hard way; however, as it says in Scripture, "Whatever you do, work heartily,

PROVERBS 13:11

Wealth gained by dishonesty
will be diminished, but he who
gathers by labor will increase.

COLOSSIANS 3:23-24

And whatever you do, do it
heartily, as to the Lord and
not to men, knowing that from
the Lord you will receive the
reward of the inheritance; for
you serve the Lord Christ.

PROVERBS 12:22

Lying lips are an abomination
to the LORD, but they that
deal truthfully are His delight.

PSALMS 24:4-5

He who has clean hands and a pure heart, who has not lifted up his soul to an idol, nor sworn deceitfully, he shall receive blessing from the LORD, and righteousness from the God of his salvation.

as for the Lord and not for men." (Colossians 3:23) As you grow, you'll learn that all the bad experiences you've had have been part of God's plan. He has guided you toward making good business decisions. If a man came to me now, offering me stolen tires, I would turn him away. I learned this lesson the hard way, thanks to God's infinite patience and forgiveness.

Honesty will take you far. It will save you from loss, pain, and setbacks. Trust that God will grant you favor. The Lord has the power to shift your company from a state of lack to a place of abundance, whether you are running a small business or a big corporation. I learned my lesson, that I don't have to purchase stolen tires, because God allowed tire manufacturers to call me and give me a discounted price on their inventory of brands they no longer want to stock or sell.

Your reputation depends on your customer's belief and trust in your business, so don't ruin it with deceit.

I want you to know that I didn't recover from setbacks because I'm the businessman of the year; it's because my Father in Heaven loves me, and even when I do wrong, his love for me doesn't change. God always gives us second chances. Let me be clear that I don't take God's grace for granted, pretending that I have plenty of time to do what's right. The time is now. In business, losses are expensive. Delight yourself in God, put your past mistakes behind you, and continue to press forward, doing business God's Way.

When you do business right, you set an example for other Kingdom businesspeople that serving God will soon pay off. If you've done wrong in business, all you have to do is admit your wrongdoing and repent. Everyone makes poor choices, but your failure doesn't define you. Failure is never final because God's grace is sufficient. Our God of mercy will put your mistakes behind you and allow you to enjoy a greater comeback than you could ever imagine.

Listen to God's Lessons

EZEKIEL 18:32

(Pastor Grier's Scripture Interpretation) For I get no pleasure in the death of your business, saith the Lord GOD; therefore turn from your wicked ways and live in prosperity.

I recently let a friend of mine read the first draft of this chapter in my book. He drives a truck, and he asked how I felt about purchasing stolen tires to save money. I knew that he'd be able to relate to my experiences with stolen tires, so I handed him my tablet.

As he read my manuscript, he said, "You know, I could have purchased some stolen tires and saved $1,000 today. I used to buy stolen tires a lot to save money. But every time I did, God would always make me pay them back. I was always breaking down on the side of the road. My tires would blow out at the worst times, and I would eventually have to pay more money than I'd saved just to get my truck repaired. The devil would tempt me with saving on a set of tires, and then I'd pay many times that amount to fix everything. It was like the stolen tires were cursed."

Blessed is the man who trusts in the Lord in all things, and who does not respect the proud nor those who turn aside to lies.

I remember at one point, my friend had to give up on his business because of all the terrible luck he was having. But it was just God teaching him a lesson, like He had done for me. Once my friend decided to listen to God, things began to get better. His credit was restored, and he was able to start his business again. God doesn't want Kingdom people to give up on their dreams, but He also wants you to live according to His plan. Sometimes the Lord just needs to teach you a lesson to keep you from falling for Satan's tricks. Once you return to God's path, ask for forgiveness; then everything Satan stole from you, you will get it back tenfold.

My friend decided to buy a new set of tires from me that day. Even though they were more expensive than the stolen tires he could have gotten, he told me, "I know that God will reward me in abundance for getting my tires from a legitimate business that does things God's way."

The Responsibility of Forgiveness

When you do wrong and you pray to God for His grace, He will show you mercy, but you have a responsibility for the forgiveness that you receive. It is up to you to make better choices in the future. If God forgives you and then you sin again or continue to make poor choices, He may not show you so much grace the next time.

Think about it this way. What if you did something to hurt your spouse and then asked them for forgiveness? If you were truly contrite, and you promised never to commit the same wrong against them again, you could reasonably

PHILIPPIANS 3:13-14

Brethren, I do not count myself to
have apprehended; but one thing
I do, forgetting those things which
are behind and reaching forward to
those things which are ahead, I press
toward the goal for the prize of the
upward call of God in Christ Jesus.

EZEKIEL 18:21-22

But if a wicked man turns from all
his sins which he has committed,
keeps all My statutes, and does
what is lawful and right, he shall
surely live; he shall not die. None
of the transgressions which he has
committed shall be remembered
against him; because of the
righteousness which he has done,
he shall live.

PSALMS 51:10

Create in me a clean
heart, O God, and renew a
steadfast spirit within me.

expect them to show you grace. However, if you received their forgiveness, and then you went out and committed the same hurtful actions against them, you would be a fool to expect them to pardon you a second time.

In the same way, God knows that we are all fallible, and yet if we keep making the same mistakes over and over, He will not reward us for this. Instead, He will execute tough love. He will teach us harder and harder lessons each time we sin, until we come back to the right path. Still, God has eternal patience. God is our Father, and He wants us to prosper. I'm a father too. I never chastised my kids because I wanted them to suffer; instead, I did it because I love them and want what's best for them. In Hebrews 12:6: "For whom the Lord loves He chastens, and scourges everyone He calls His son." God chastised me and my friend, the trucker, just to get us on the right path. God is love, and He will show us endless mercy. He will always accept and forgive us, but he wants us to return to the light so we can make money and prosper His way.

Never Cheat Your Employees

Our true character is most transparent when we are placed in a position of power. When I first started my business, I researched what would be a decent pay for my employees based on their job position and previous work experience, as well as our location. I strongly feel that as Kingdom business owners, we should want to be fair and treat people how we would want to be treated. I've seen so many people work for companies that

PSALMS 37:4

Delight yourself also in the LORD, and He shall give you the desires of your heart.

PROVERBS 3:27

Do not withhold good from those to whom it is due, when it is in the power of your hand to do so.

MATTHEW 25:23

His lord said to him, "Well done, good and faithful servant; you have been faithful over a few things, I will make you ruler over many things. Enter into the joy of your lord."

underpay them, not because the company can't afford to give them a fair wage, but because the company owner feels that they can get away with it. I believe in my heart that the way we treat our employees shows the measure of our integrity. God watches how we do business to see if he can trust us to give us more. Here is what the Scriptures say:

I know you may be thinking, "Are so many business owners really thieves?" According to PushBlack Finance, wage theft in the US affects more people than every other form of theft, costing hard-working Americans billions of dollars every year.[2] That's more than robbery and burglary combined. There are many forms of wage theft, such as not being fairly compensated, not getting overtime after 40 hours, being forced to work before clocking in, working while on break, and not being allowed breaks at all. Not only is this ungodly, it is illegal.

> Everyone makes poor choices, but your failure doesn't define you. Failure is never final because God's grace is sufficient.

When an employee is underpaid, it leaves them feeling stressed, overwhelmed, and unappreciated. Their good work ethic soon dwindles. I know we're not required to save the world; however, when we're prospering financially in our business, let's reach out to those whom God has placed in our care. A business owner with a good loving heart will want to build up their team, just as God builds up their business.

I believe that love is compassion in action: "But whoever has this world's goods, and sees his brother in need, and shuts up his heart from him, how does the love of God abide in him?" (1 John

2.   Chatman, Shiavon. "Stolen Wages Cost Low Income Workers Billions Each Year." PushBlack Finance, September 9 2021, pushblackfinance.com/news/stolen-wages-cost-low-income-workers-billions-each-year.

1 CORINTHIANS 15:10

But by the grace of God, I
am what I am, and His grace
toward me was not in vain;
but I labored more abundantly
than all of them; yet not I, but
the grace of God which was
with me.

ISAIAH 43:18-19

Do not remember the former things,
nor consider the things of old. Behold,
I will do a new thing, now it shall
spring forth; shall you not know
it? I will even make a road in the
wilderness and rivers in the desert.

1 PETER 2:9

But you are a chosen generation, a
royal priesthood, a holy nation, His
own special people, that you may
proclaim the praises of Him who
called you out of darkness into His
marvelous light.

3:17) I believe when we give from our heart and treat our team fairly, God will give us more than we can ask for: "Give, and it will be given to you. A good measure, pressed down, shaken together, and running over will be put into your bosom. For with the same measure that you use, it will be measured back to you." (Luke 6:38).

Many business owners contend that they are only required to pay minimum wage, which allows them to take the rest of the profits. I know that this is allowable by US law, but as Jeremiah 22:13 tells us, "Woe to him who builds his house by unrighteousness and his chambers by injustice, who uses his neighbor's service without wages and gives him nothing for his work." There is no law that should supersede God's law. If your business can afford to do more for your employees and continue to prosper, I recommend that you increase their compensation accordingly. If you can't afford to pay your employees more, but you really desire to do so, I pray that God counts your desire as righteous and that your business prospers because of your heart's desire to bless others. Do good and good will come back to you.

Nowhere in America today can a minimum-wage worker afford a two-bedroom apartment. Even worse, 93% of full-time workers can barely afford a one-bedroom apartment. This is sad but true, but it's not because our businesses and corporations are suffering — it's pure greed. Kingdom businessmen and businesswomen must be different. We must not operate from greed. Don't allow greed and the love of money to get between your relationship with God and the Kingdom responsibilities that He requires of you.

Pastor Grier's Integrity Prayer for Your Business

Dear kind and heavenly Father. I know I haven't always done what's right, but I'm thankful for Your grace and mercy. Continue to teach me how to let my business be a good representation of You. Allow me to be an honest businessman even when no one else but You is watching. Give me the resources to treat my team fairly as we grow together. Continue to bless my business abundantly, and every time You bless me, remind me to be a blessing to my team, my customers, my family, my community, and my country.

Amen.

3

COUNT THE TRUE
COST

CHAPTER 3

Count the True Cost

Return on Investment

When you work for yourself, you need to make sure that you count the true cost of operating your business. Why? Because you want to make sure that you're getting a good return on your investment (ROI), and not taking a loss. When you have a good ROI, it means that your business is earning a profit in a timely manner. For your business to be successful, you need to know what you're investing versus what you will get in return. In short, are you gaining or losing? Thoroughly evaluate your business to be certain that you will prosper.

The Bible says, "Count the cost." (Luke 14:28) Let me add a second component to this command, which is essential for Kingdom business owners:

Prosperity for Kingdom men and women is not solely defined by how much we profit financially. Yes, we want to prosper — that's the ultimate goal in business. However, we must not base our ROI on financial gain alone. Our business success comes from making money God's Way and trusting Him for an abundant return.

There are several factors that will allow you to count the true cost and determine whether everything adds up. I know some of you may be saying, "What else can my business cost me other than a financial loss or gain?"

I'm going to ask you several questions, and I'm going to let you decide whether your business is giving you a good ROI from a Kingdom perspective:

- Is your business causing you to miss your kids' sports events, recitals, and other important family moments? Do you think it's a good return on your investment to be absent from your kids' lives?
- Is your business causing you to miss too many Sunday services? Do you think it's a good return on your investment to allow your Christian values to weaken?
- Are you always stressed, overwhelmed, and on the verge of snapping? Do you think it's a good return on your investment to lose your peace of mind?

I've lost count of the number of business owners who have told me, "I'm financially stable, but mentally I'm overwhelmed. I'm putting all my energy into my business, and I don't have time to raise my kids." I've been there myself, and I know the true cost. I know the cost of being so stretched that you don't have time for your family. I know the cost of being so exhausted that you are drained mentally, emotionally, physically, and spiritually.

I can tell you from experience that financial success alone does not equal a good ROI for your business. I've learned the hard way that when you run your business from this place of imbalance, you will be unable to make money God's Way or live according to His Word.

This is why we as Kingdom people don't base our return on just money alone. Let me share with you the way God says it: "The blessing of the Lord makes you rich, but it adds no sorrow." (Proverbs 10:22) If your business interferes with your family, your kids, and ultimately your marriage, it will add sorrow to your life. This is not what God wants for you. The Scriptures tell us, "What God has joined together, let nothing put asunder." (Mark 10:9) In other words, your business shouldn't ever interfere with your marriage. God wants your family to prosper so that the Kingdom may prosper. If your business is leading you toward divorce, then ask yourself, are you getting a good ROI? As a true Kingdom person, you must seek to get more from your business than money, otherwise Satan will use this as an opportunity to ruin other areas of your life. If money is your sole desire, then Satan already has his foot in your door, and he's just waiting for the opportunity to push it open and destroy you. The Scriptures warn us against this kind of greed: "For the love of money is the root of all evil, for which some have strayed from the faith in their greediness and have pierced themselves through with many sorrows." (1 Timothy 6:10)

God will not have us walking around ignorant of Satan schemes (1 Thessalonians 4:13). If you find that you're not getting what God wants you

Prosperity for Kingdom men and women is not solely defined by how much we profit financially.

LUKE 14:28

For which of you, intending to build a tower, does not sit down first and count the cost, whether he has enough to finish it?

PROVERBS 10:22

The blessing of the Lord makes one rich, and He adds no sorrow with it.

to have, stop and count the cost. Something is not adding up. The Scriptures tell us that "The peace of God, which surpasses all understanding, will guard your hearts and minds through Christ Jesus." (Philippians 4:7) If your business is stealing your peace, you either need to make adjustments to the way that you are working, or you need to close or sell your business.

Some businesses will keep you up all night. You're always on the go, always working. Some nights you work until 4:00 a.m. You rarely see your kids. You rely on pills to get to sleep. If this is you, and your business is robbing you of your sleep, then it is also robbing you of your health. I've been a person who would work round the clock, seven days a week. I was mentally and physically drained, and I was indirectly ruining my health. I was operating my business contrary to God's Word. The Scriptures tell us, "Beloved, I pray that you may prosper in all things and be in health, just as your soul prospers." (3 John 2:2) If your business is hijacking your health, then you're not getting a good return on your investment.

> **As a true Kingdom person, you must seek to get more from your business than money, otherwise Satan will use this as an opportunity to ruin other areas of your life.**

I want business owners to understand that owning a business can require a lot of time when you're in the building stage. You have limited capital, you have to wear many hats, and if you're not careful, Satan can drain you of your strength and spirit. God wants us to make our health a priority, no matter how busy our business is. Satan wants us to make money our only priority; in that way, our health will deteriorate. If we sicken or die, Satan doesn't have to worry about us sharing

God's Word and building the Kingdom. Our bodies are very important to God. In the Old Testament, He even tells us what we should and shouldn't eat. In the New Testament, the Scriptures tell us, "I beseech you therefore, brethren, by the mercies of God, that you present your bodies a living sacrifice, holy, acceptable to God, which is your reasonable service." (Romans 12:1) Maintaining good health is reasonable for you to accomplish. Don't compromise or neglect your health for financial freedom — it is not a good return on your investment, and it is not doing business God's Way.

When you measure the true cost of running your business, you examine the cost as a whole, counting every area of your life. If your business is negatively affecting other aspects of your life, you must ask yourself, "Is this what God has for me? Or do I need to make some changes? Should I hire a better team? Should I reallocate some of my duties to other employees so I have the time to raise my children?"

When you look at the cost as a whole, you may recognize that your business has a poor ROI, even if it is financially profitable. To count the true cost, ask yourself:

- Am I losing my kids to the streets?
- Am I losing my marriage to divorce?
- Am I losing my health to poor diet and no sleep?
- Am I losing the joy I once had for my business to stress and overwhelm?

If you answered "yes" to any of these questions, you have a poor ROI, regardless of how much money you make. This is a sign that you need to reevaluate your business plan. Take time to sit down and count the true costs of operating your business. It's important for Kingdom business owners to

Bring all the tithes into the storehouse, that there may be food in My house, and try Me now in this," says the Lord of hosts. "If I will not open for you the windows of Heaven and pour out for you such blessing that there will not be room enough to receive it. And I will rebuke the devourer for your sakes, so that he will not destroy the fruit of your ground, nor shall the vine fail to bear fruit for you in the field.

understand that we can always make money, but we can't lose our family, our peace of mind, or our Christian values in the money-making process.

Money Can't Raise Kids

As Kingdom business owners, we must understand that our family needs our time, and not just our financial support. Being financially responsible and profitable isn't the only measure of success. If we are so dedicated to our work that we neglect our kids and our marriage, we are throwing ourselves into a state of imbalance. This gives Satan an invitation to enter our homes and break us down.

When I was a younger man, my daughter asked me many times to attend her games and events. I missed plenty. I thought it was enough that my wife was in the audience. I justified my absence by telling myself that I was busy being the breadwinner, so my money was attending my daughter's events in my place. My daughter is a smart young woman, and she saw through this excuse. One day, she told me, "Dad, you never come to see my games, and I would really like both you and mom to be there." I felt terrible. I knew she was right. Kids need their parents' time and attention. At the end of the day, kids will remember the quality time that their parents spend with them, not the money that their parents spend on them.

"Making money God's Way" is all about balance. On the one hand, we need to avoid being financially irresponsible, i.e., we must be careful with debt. But on the other hand, we need to avoid being miserly, i.e., we should be generous with the time and attention we give to our family and friends. We must cherish our health and our loved ones because when they're gone, we'll miss them dearly, and money can't bring them back.

I remember a conversation I had with my cousin several years ago. I was comparing my upbringing to his life growing up as a child. I said, "Cuz, you and your brothers had a pretty good life. Your dad had a good business and pretty much gave you the world. Y'all had everything. You didn't really have financial struggles growing up. I remember y'all got just about everything you wanted. Every time Nike's came out, y'all had the latest name brand shoes. Y'all had name brand clothes. Man, I didn't get any name brand items until I was in high school when I worked a summer job. You had that stuff when you were in elementary and middle school. I mean, your dad was great."

My cousin looked at me and shook his head. He said to me, "Cuz, you were on the outside looking in. What you saw looked like my dad was great. Of course, my dad gave us everything financially. We had all the shoes and clothes we needed. Whatever stuff we wanted, our dad provided it for us. But dad still didn't give me everything that I needed. Man, you may not believe this, but you got more from your dad than I did. Did you know that during all those years I played basketball and football, my dad never went to a single game? Do you know how hurtful that is? I would look out at the audience every game, hoping that maybe this time my dad made it, and then I'd feel disappointed when I saw that he wasn't there. Yeah, my dad gave me what I wanted financially, but he didn't give me his time. He was never around. He was always busy making money. I didn't get his support when I most needed it. That's one of the reasons why I make it my business to be at most of my son's football and basketball games. I try to make it to

PROVERBS 3:9-10

Honor the Lord with your possessions, and with the firstfruits of all your increase; so your barns will be filled with plenty, and your vats will overflow with new wine.

ROMANS 11:16

For if the firstfruit is holy, the rest is also holy; and if the root is holy, so are the branches.

his practices as well because I know firsthand how hurtful it is to go through life without seeing your dad in the audience. So yeah, it looked like we had everything, but we didn't have the most important thing, which was our dad's attention and support."

The Scriptures say in 1 Timothy 5:8, "But if anyone does not provide for his own, and especially for those of his household, he has denied the faith and is worse than an unbeliever." I believe that in this verse, the word "provide" doesn't stop at money, clothes, and shoes. I believe we're called and obligated to provide whatever our family needs. This includes our time, love, patience, training, and everything God has equipped us to give our children. When we raise our kids, we should never try to substitute our time with money. God has called us to train up our children in the right way, and training requires time.

Partner with God

In business, we're eager to make investments to gain a profit. We invest in stocks, bonds, and Bitcoins, but many of us are slow to invest in the Kingdom. Instead of giving ourselves over to worldly matters, we must partner with God.

The decision to partner with God is one of the best investments you will make as a business owner. Partnership is two or more parties coming together to work toward a common goal. Your contribution to the partnership includes tithing 10%. When you give God your first 10%, you are letting Him know that you trust Him to bless you with the remaining 90%.

Let's explore the benefits of partnering with God. In the book of Malachi 3:10, God says,

EZEKIEL 44:30

Give God the firstfruits, and every oblation of all that He may cause the blessing to rest in your house.

"Bring all the tithes into the storehouse, that there may be food in My house." God is asking for 10% of your business profits, i.e., the first fruit offering. When you give Him 10%, He will provide you with the other 90%. This partnership is unlike any other, in that most partners want a 50/50 split. God is different. Even though He gives you the power to get wealth, and He has given you 100% of what you have, He still only asks that you remember Him for 10% to build the Kingdom of Heaven. What a deal! When God is your partner, you will succeed in what you set out to do. Jesus said in John 15:5, "I am the vine, you are the branches. He who abides in Me, and I in him, bears much fruit; for without Me you can do nothing."

> We must cherish our health and our loved ones because when they're gone, we'll miss them dearly, and money can't bring them back.

The Significance of Tithes

Tithes keep the Kingdom from starving. In Malachi 3:10–11, God says, "I will open you the windows of Heaven, and pour you out a blessing, that there shall not be room enough to receive it. And I will rebuke the devourer for your sakes, and he shall not destroy the fruits of your ground; neither shall your vine cast her fruit before the time in the field." When you tithe, God will pour you out a blessing that your cup will begin to run over. You won't even have enough room to receive the blessing He will bestow upon your life, your business, your children, and your body. Hallelujah, glory to God! There is no greater partner to invest with. Let me tell you something, if Coca-Cola or another Fortune 500 company offered this deal, many of us would jump at the chance to give them 10% of our increase. What business owners do you know that wouldn't go for this opportunity? After all, every one of us wants our business to prosper.

In Malachi 3:11, God says, "I will rebuke the devourer for your sakes." A devourer is anything that's set out to destroy you, and if it can tear you down, it will also tear down your business. This includes pandemics, recessions, periods of inflation, haters, lazy employees, competitors, and liars that are eager to ruin your business. God will rebuke your devourer, meaning that your haters can't harm you. Your competition can't close you down. The recession won't affect you. The pandemic is beneath you. God will rebuke and bind anything that sets out to harm you. Why? Because you have committed to partner with the Lord almighty by sowing your firstfruits to build God's Kingdom.

I call this partnership "The Business Protection Plan." When you partner with God and sow into the Kingdom by tithing 10%, God gives you protection, favor, and overflow. This partnership provides many benefits. Most importantly, it allows you to fulfill your duties as a Kingdom business owner. You can be business driven, but still be Kingdom living.

Why We Should Tithe Our 10%

Now, you may ask, "Why does it matter if I invest 10% in God?"

It matters because Matthew 6:21 tells us, "Where your treasure is, there will your heart be also." The Scriptures say in 1 Samuel 16:7, "Man looks at the outward appearance, but the Lord looks at the heart." God judges people based on what is in their heart. He looks at your heart, and He knows what you feel and believe within. He can tell how committed you are to Him, and He only wants to partner with people who are serious about serving the Kingdom. That's why it matters. I know this firsthand. For many years, I said, "Lord, I'm going to tithe when my finances begin to overflow, but right now I don't have much." What I didn't understand was that Malachi 3:10 is a cause-and-effect statement. When you pay your tithes with whatever you have, God will open up the windows of Heaven and pour you out a blessing in such abundance that you won't even have room enough to receive it. However, you won't get that bountiful effect until you initiate the cause.

Some of you might be thinking, "Well, I'm going to start tithing when I start making six figures. I need to work my way up to the top first."

I used to say that myself. I put off tithing as long as I could, and then I wondered why my business was at a standstill. I waited and waited, but my business never reached my expectations. I received no growth and no overflow. You mustn't procrastinate, giving God empty promises that you will start paying your tithes when you become a millionaire. If you genuinely feel that tithing is too hard, you need to ask yourself, "Do I truly hold God within my heart?" If you don't want to put any money into the Kingdom, then your heart is not with the Kingdom. If you wait to invest in the Kingdom of God until you have all the money in the world, God will turn you down. He doesn't want that type of

> **The decision to partner with God is one of the best investments you will make as a business owner.**

partnership. The Scriptures say, "Be faithful for a few things and I'll make you ruler over many." (Matthew 25:21) Start with the little that you have, and watch God multiply the little into greater and greater amounts. Luke 16:10-11 tells us, "Whoever can be trusted with very little can also be trusted with much, and whoever is dishonest with very little will also be dishonest with much. So if you have not been trustworthy in handling worldly wealth, who will trust you with true riches?" We must be faithful to God as it relates to money. Being obedient to tithing will reap blessings. You must believe that you will not fail when you are obedient to God, even when you have little to give Him.

When you tithe, God will raise you up. He will elevate you. He will open up doors for you and send you all the business that you need. Don't let money separate you from God and your Kingdom values. Paul said, "For I am persuaded that neither death nor life, nor angels nor principalities nor powers, nor things present nor things to come, nor height nor depth, nor any other created thing, shall be able to separate us from the love of God which is in Christ Jesus our Lord."

Some of you may be worrying, "Lord, I'm afraid I may go bankrupt when I start tithing. If I give you 10%, I don't see how You will be able to repay me with 90%. I'm on a tight budget; I can't partner right now."

If you feel this way, let me be honest with you — don't partner with God. You should never partner with someone in business that you don't trust. If you don't trust God, if you don't believe in what He says, then don't ask Him to be your partner.

This is what I believe about God. Psalm 37:25 says, "I have not seen the righteous forsaken, nor his descendants begging bread." Psalm 23 says, "The Lord is my shepherd, I shall not want." Romans 11:16 tells us, "For if the firstfruit is holy, the rest is also holy; and if the root is holy, so are the branches." Psalm 40:4 says, "Blessed is that man who makes the Lord his trust, and does not respect the proud, nor turn aside to lies."

Many of us are eager to partner with corporations and other worldly companies, and yet we're afraid to partner with God. I'm not implying you shouldn't invest in other opportunities, but the Kingdom must always be your priority. Why be afraid to partner with the One who created the world? Give your trust to God. Let me reassure you that unlike other investments, the Kingdom of God is undefeated and has never lost. Psalms 24:1 says, "The earth is the Lord's, and all its fullness, the world and those who dwell therein." Everything here belongs to God, so why not partner with the One who oversees all things? In my opinion, corporate investments are great, but they're the middleman. It's better for my business to cut out the middleman and deal first with my Father in Heaven. Pray to God to increase your faith in Him so you can partner with Him without fear. Be a blessing to the Kingdom and be a successful business leader while doing so. That is the best business protection plan you can invest in.

Trust God As Your Partner

Several years ago, an old classmate of mine got a tire from me and didn't pay me. Seven months later, I saw him again beside the road with another flat tire. He was walking in the heavy rain, carrying his tire to a shop.

God told me, "Pick him up."

PROVERBS 3:5-6

Trust in the Lord with all your heart, and lean not on your own understanding. In all your ways acknowledge Him, and He shall direct your paths.

PSALMS 34:8

Oh, taste and see that the Lord is good. Blessed is the man who trusts in Him!

I said, "Oh no, God. Please don't make me. That dude didn't pay me the last time. It's not fair to me to give him a free ride now."

I continued down the road for a few miles, but it was raining so hard that God softened my heart and compelled me to turn around and go help him out. I pulled up beside him and asked him where he was going. He told me he was walking to a shop that was down the road from mine. He explained that he didn't feel comfortable coming to me because he already owed me, and he had just enough money for his current situation. I told him not to worry about it. I took him to my shop and replaced his tire. He didn't have the full amount for the second tire, but I took another chance. He explained to me that he was having a really tough time. He had not forgotten that he owed me, and he assured me that he would repay me. I wasn't expecting him to reimburse me because it had been so long, but the next week, he paid me back for everything. He not only gave me what he owed me for the second tire, but he also settled

When you tithe, God will pour you out a blessing that your cup will begin to run over

up his past debt. That situation taught me that I must trust God even when it doesn't feel right, even when everything in my nature is telling me no. Since I trusted God and showed my old classmate compassion, God made sure that I received what was owed to me. Had I not been obedient to God, I would have lost a customer, I wouldn't have been paid for the second tire he purchased, and I might never have been compensated for the previous bill he owed me. God encouraged me to help this man during the most difficult time in his life, and I believe that's ultimately why he repaid me.

The lesson is this: even when every fibre of your being tells you to turn your back on someone,

DEUTERONOMY 8:18

You shall remember the Lord your God, for it is He who gives you power to get wealth, that He may establish His covenant, which He swore to your fathers, as it is this day.

you must trust God. He is your partner. Obey Him, believe His words, and have faith in the path that He is directing you along.

Here is another story. It was October 2016. God gave me a vision to expand my business into selling dirt bikes and ATVs. Unfortunately, I couldn't afford to purchase this inventory outright, and I didn't have enough credit to finance it. In November 2016, I went ahead and filled out the application to become a dealer, but I didn't have the credit or finances to stock the inventory. I thought I would never have the opportunity to pursue this dream. Over time, I forgot about it. Then in March 2020, at the beginning of the pandemic, the bank called me and gave me the green light to buy the inventory I needed. God even placed a financial institution in my path that would finance my customers for $50 down with no credit check to make sure that I could sell my inventory.

While walking one day, I looked up to heaven in tears and said, "God, you didn't forget about me, even when I sometimes had forgotten about you." God waited three and a half years to intercede on my behalf to make this vision come to fruition, but He showed up at the right time and helped me in the midst of the pandemic. I want to encourage business owners, if God gives you a vision for your business and it looks like it's not going to happen, don't worry — continue to trust God as your partner. He may not come at your time, but He'll come at His time, and His time is always the right time. It's a blessing to have a partner who is working for you and with you. God will open up Heaven and pour you out a blessing that you won't even have room enough to receive. It could be two or three years for your vision to manifest, but no matter how long it takes, trust God. He is your partner, and He will come through.

Pastor Grier's Partnership Prayer for Your Business

Dear kind and heavenly Father. I've decided to partner with You not because I want to bribe You into giving me the blessing of prosperity, but because I know that everything that I have belongs to You. It is You that gives me power to get wealth. Lord, I trust Your decisions concerning myself and my business. Help me to believe in You even when the light seems dim. Help me to believe in You even when my business is in its slow season. Help me to believe in You when all my bills are due. But most importantly, show me that our partnership is a win-win for both of us: Not only is it valuable for me financially, but it's also valuable to You for Your Kingdom.

Amen.

4

**BE INDEBTED TO NO
ONE EXCEPT TO ONE
ANOTHER IN LOVE**

CHAPTER 4

Be Indebted to No One Except to One Another in Love

My Wedding Story

Many years back, my wife and I were planning our wedding. We had a budget of $15,000 for everything. That was a lot of money, and I didn't know how I was going to pay it without going into debt. I prayed to God for help, and God said to me, "Winston, you're going to get married, and you're not going to have to borrow a dime."

We knew that we had to pay everything in full no later than thirty days before the date. The deadline was fast approaching, and soon, our wedding day was only two months away. By then, my wife and I had managed to pay $3,000 for what we owed, but we still had $12,000 left. We had to pay for the decorator, the wedding venue, and everything else, and we only had a month to do it. We didn't know how we were going to make those payments.

My wife was worried. She told me, "Winston, I think we're going to have to get a loan. It's going to be too hard for us to pay that off in just a month."

I shook my head and said, "Babe, when I proposed to you, God told me that I wouldn't have to get a loan. I've got to trust God."

I put my faith in God, and He came through for me. That week, I earned nearly $7,000. Within a month, I made more than $25,000. It was the most money I'd ever earned in my business up to that point. God opened up the wonders of Heaven for my wife and me. Had I gone out and gotten a loan, I would have never had the opportunity to see God's work.

I told God, "Lord, I trust in You; do not let me be put to shame." Even though getting that money seemed impossible, I put my faith in God, and He answered my prayers. He sent more people than ever to my business, and He made sure that I did amazing numbers throughout that month. My phone calls, my road calls, and my tire sales all increased.

Before that month, my wife and I had planned our honeymoon in Myrtle Beach, SC. It was not our first choice, but it was what we could afford. We didn't have the money for airfare, so we had to pick a nearby honeymoon destination that we could drive to. But God did so much for us that in about six weeks, we were able to book a honeymoon in Florida. God made sure that we didn't have to drive. We got to fly there, and we had enough money left over to hire a chauffeur. Not only that, but we were able to extend our vacation to a full week, when we were originally planning to stay only three days.

PROVERBS 3:9–10

Honor the LORD with your wealth and with the firstfruits of all your harvest; then your barns will be filled with plenty, and your vats will overflow with new wine.

God opened up that door to us, and He will do the same for you in your business. If you trust God and don't fall for Satan's schemes, the Lord will show up for you. But He can't show up if you decide that you don't need Him. If I had gotten a loan to pay for my wedding, there would have been no reason for God to manifest for me because I would have already taken the matter into my own hands.

God's Job Is to Do the Impossible

When you look at your financial situation and say, "There's no way that I can come up with this kind of money in a month's time," you may be right — you can't do it, but God can. Remember, you're not in business by yourself. You have a partner in God. That's why it has to be done God's Way. When you can't accomplish something by yourself, you must lean on your partner — He can make it happen. It doesn't help you to partner with God if you don't allow Him to do what He does best. God performs miracles. When He is in control, there's nothing that's too hard for Him. He built the universe in seven days, so He can change your financial situation overnight. You see, what seemed impossible to me when I was planning my wedding was nothing for God. It was easy for Him. But I had to trust that He was going to deliver. My job was to put my faith in God; once I did that, He came through for me and made sure that I didn't go into debt.

As a business owner, I've had times when I put myself into hardship because I didn't fully trust in God's ability to manifest for me. I overspent until

I ruined my credit rating, and I allowed predatory lenders to loan me money. After years of struggling in this way, I finally realized what I was doing wrong — I was trying to do everything by myself. That's what got me tricked into financial bondage. I got into debt because I didn't allow God to do His part. I learned that God wants nothing more than for Kingdom people to prosper. When we partner with God, He won't let us fail.

The Evils of Working Capital Loans

I want you to be wary of working capital loans. They may seem like heavenly intercession, but in reality, they are often one of Satan's schemes. With a working capital loan, your business can be approved based on your business income. These lenders don't pull your credit report to check your credit. The only thing they look at are your numbers. Working capital loans are designed to target people and businesses that don't have good credit.

If you don't have good credit, and someone reaches out to you for a business loan opportunity, your ears will be open to that. Everyone in business is looking for ways to get capital, but the way a working capital loan is designed, you will never come out ahead. The only people that make money from the deal are the people that give the loan.

When I took out a working capital loan, I borrowed $65,000, and I had to pay back $95,000 at $647 a day. The lender drafted the money right out of my business checking account every day. Not only that, but I had to repay the loan plus interest in under a year. So, with that working capital loan, I gave away $30,000 of my potential profit. They also charged me a $1,350 "setup" fee, which they took out of my loan amount. My back was up against the wall because of my bad credit, and they knew that I didn't have the leverage to push back against those kinds of usurious fees. They didn't even give me a week to organize my finances so I could make my first payment. They debited the first payment out of my account the very next day. Meanwhile, I also had overhead expenses, business expenses, and payroll, so everyone was earning money except for me, the business owner.

God performs miracles. When He is in control, there's nothing that's too hard for Him.

The only thing a working capital loan does is make you dig a hole for yourself. Because after you finish paying, guess what? You're often in such bad financial straits that you have to go back and get another working capital loan. It keeps you trapped in a cycle of financial dependence.

Business-Friendly Working Capital Loans

There are a few working capital loans that are business friendly, such as those from PayPal and Square. At least at the time of this writing, these working capital loans offer some reasonable interest rates for business owners with poor credit. They are set up to take a low percentage from each of your credit card transactions until you settle your account. The upside of this loan is that if your business doesn't make anything that day or that week, you don't pay anything. This is unlike the working capital loans I took out, where I still had to repay the loan daily, whether my business made money or not. These newer types of loans may be the best option if you have bad credit and don't have any other choice. Regardless, I recommend that you always seek God first for a way out, rather than seeking out a lender for a high interest loan.

The Evils of Title Loans

Another type of predatory loan is a title loan. In the past, I borrowed money from title places because of my bad credit. I needed money to help me purchase inventory because so much of my daily income was going to pay off my working capital loans. I thought the title loan would help me float the boat, but it was actually one of the worst financial decisions I made.

I borrowed $2,500 from a title loan, and I had to repay at least the minimum amount each month, which in my case was $200. So long as you pay the minimum, they renew your loan. However, here's the lesson I learned: When you're in a bad financial situation, it's always tempting to pay the minimum and no more. I kept paying the minimum every month, but after three years, I realized that I had given the lending company $7,500. Even worse than that, I still owed the original $2,500 on top of the $7,500 I'd paid in interest. So, I borrowed $2,500, and I paid back $10,000 over three years.

Whatever inventory I'd bought with the original $2,500 loan wasn't worth it. At the end of those three years, I was in worse shape than I had been in before I took the title loan. I can guarantee that I didn't earn $10,000 from my $2,500 investment.

ROMANS 13:8

Be indebted to no one, except to one another in love. For he who loves his neighbor has fulfilled the law.

PROVERBS 21:5

The plans of the diligent lead surely to plenty, but those of everyone who is hasty, surely to poverty.

PROVERBS 13:16

Every prudent man acts with knowledge, but a fool lays open his folly.

These kinds of predatory loans are designed to hinder your business growth and keep you in debt. They keep you stressed out and overwhelmed, and they force you to stay in financial bondage. The more debt you incur, the more likely you are to incur further debt. It is a vicious cycle.

Satan's Goal Is to Keep You in Financial Bondage

Satan's ultimate goal is to keep you in bondage. If he can keep you down, he doesn't have to worry about you contributing to the Kingdom and preaching about how good God is. The companies that offer predatory loans dress them up in a way that makes them look so appealing. They try to trick you into thinking that you will get lots of extra cash and your life will be so much easier. The approval process is often only twenty-four hours. They tell you, "Just imagine it. Within the space of one day, you could be $50,000 richer."

These companies have salesmen who know exactly what to say, and it's no coincidence that they have your number. There are third parties that sell your information to these predatory lenders. They have a detailed profile on you. Maybe you have applied for a business loan from a reputable lender, and you didn't get approved. Once you leave, that lender sells your information, where it is bought by predatory lending companies. These companies now know your situation, and they know that you need this cash right away. They don't target people with an 800 credit score. They target people who have already been rejected for business loans.

Title loan and working capital companies are persistent. They will call you and send you junk mail every week. Working capital lenders will tempt you with a $50,000 loan when the loan you were originally rejected for was only $15,000. They know your pain points. They are fully aware that you can't go anywhere else due to your credit score. They know that you have the income to pay back the loan principal plus interest. They don't care how you get them their money, and they aren't worried about you paying them because they draft the money directly out of your account. Even worse, if you default on your loan payments, they will send you to collection, and they know that this will make your credit score drop even more, making you even more vulnerable in the future.

These are what I call Satanic strategies. They are loans designed to hurt people. I believe there is such a thing as good debt and bad debt. These predatory loans are what I call horrible debt. It's a terrible position to put your business in, not to mention yourself and your family.

You Don't Know the Future

Predatory lenders loan you money based on your future receivables. In essence, you are borrowing money based on income that you *think* you are going to make in the future. But here's the thing — you're not psychic. You don't know what you're going to make in the future. Just because you may have made $25,000 this month doesn't mean you're going to make that amount next month or the month after.

For example, none of us knew that the pandemic was going to come. I have an inflatable

HAGGAI 1:5–7

Now therefore, thus says the Lord of hosts: "Consider your ways! You have sown much, and bring in little; you eat, but do not have enough; you drink, but you are not filled with drink; you clothe yourselves, but no one is warm; and he who earns wages, earns wages to put into a bag with holes." Thus says the Lord of hosts: "Consider your ways!"

rental business in addition to my tire business, but for two years, I didn't rent any inflatables because nobody was doing events. Before the pandemic, I estimated what I thought I would make in the 2020 and 2021 summer months, but I didn't make any of that potential income.

As another example, I had a tire business that was doing about $8,000 a week for several years. Then a rival truck tire shop that was part of a national chain opened up a few miles away from me. I went from making $8,000 a week to $10,000 a month. All of a sudden, my income was a quarter of what it used to be. If I had gotten a working capital or title loan based on my receivables, I wouldn't have been able to predict that this rival company would set up shop right down the road.

You really don't know what your future income is going to be and yet with a predatory loan, you have a lender that demands payment every day. This is a big risk to take. You are paying a high interest rate, and on top of that, your income is contingent on so many unpredictable factors that you can't control, like your competition and your customer base, not to mention events like a pandemic or a recession.

The Only Way Out of Financial Bondage Is Through God

This is what I want you to consider: if it takes God to get you out of this financial bondage, why not just depend on Him for something more reasonable in the first place? God is your business partner, and you are asking Him to bail you out. You are asking, "Lord, please get me out of this mess!" And He will. But you could have just gone to your business partner in the first place and asked Him for help.

When you do things God's Way, He will always provide. You can ask Him to open up opportunities for you, to provide for you, and He will. You can't afford to put yourself into a situation of financial bondage, but even in those situations, you still have to go to God.

The Scriptures tell us in Philippians 4:6, "Be anxious for nothing, but in everything by prayer and supplication, with thanksgiving, let your requests be made known to God." So, why wait to go to God until you have put yourself in a bad situation that only He can get you out of? Why not just trust God from the start and have faith that once you make a request to Him, He will make a provision for you? In 2 Kings 4:1–7, look at the wonders that God worked:

KINGS 4:1-7

A certain woman of the wives of the sons of the prophets cried out to Elisha, saying, "Your servant my husband is dead, and you know that your servant feared the Lord. And the creditor is coming to take my two sons to be his slaves."

So Elisha said to her, "What shall I do for you? Tell me, what do you have in the house?" And she said, "Your maidservant has nothing in the house but a jar of oil."

Then he said, "Go, borrow vessels from everywhere, from all your neighbors — empty vessels; do not gather just a few. And when you have come in, you shall shut the door behind you and your sons; then pour it into all those vessels, and set aside the full ones."

So she went from him and shut the door behind her and her sons, who brought the vessels to her; and she poured it out. Now it came to pass, when the vessels were full, that she said to her son, "Bring me another vessel."

And he said to her, "There is not another vessel." So the oil ceased. Then she came and told the man of God. And he said, "Go, sell the oil and pay your debt; and you and your sons live on the rest."

The woman could have easily gotten herself into debt, but she trusted in God's ability to provide. Here the Lord took the little that she had and multiplied it so much until she had more oil than vessels. Go to God the way this woman did, and He will multiply the little that you have as well.

Debt Is Essential in Business – But Make Sure It's Good Debt

When you are in business, it is essential to use debt to your advantage. Your business won't get off the ground without financing. The important thing is not to allow debt to use you. Just like there is bad debt, there is also good debt. When you get a business loan from a bank, you will have a reasonable monthly payment with a relatively low interest rate. The bank will expect you to repay the amount in five to ten years. Compare this to a predatory loan, which requires daily payments with a high interest rate, and a repayment period of less than twelve months. Only take on debt that you can pay back within an achievable timeframe.

With good credit, I could have gotten the same $65,000 loan and paid back $600 a month, instead of $600 a day. I could have scheduled a repayment period of nine years instead of nine months. I could have paid a 5% interest rate instead of a 30% interest rate. Having good credit puts me in a better position to win. I can take advantage of good debt. It helps me build my business, and it can boost my credit score. $600 a month is good debt; $600 a day is horrible debt.

If you are considering taking out a predatory loan, ask yourself if you can really afford to pay back tens of thousands of dollars in interest in under a year. If you determine that you can comfortably earn enough in your business to pay that much money, that's God's way of telling you that you don't need a loan in the first place. And if paying back $30,000 in interest in nine months would be a hardship or impossible for you, that is God telling you to avoid this scheme. Instead, pray to God to give you the patience not to rush into debt.

Bad debt comes from the devil. It is part of Satan's plan to divert your heart and mind from your Kingdom responsibilities. Matthew 6:21 tells us, "For where your treasure is, there your heart will be also." Satan enjoys it when your heart is not with God, for he knows that he will be able to rob you of every dime you've got. Signing on with a predatory lender is choosing a sinful choice. A sinful choice is anything that doesn't align with God. But don't just take my word for it. Here is what Investopedia says:

"Predatory lending typically refers to lending practices that impose unfair, deceptive, or abusive loan terms on borrowers. In many cases, these loans carry high fees and interest rates, strip the borrower of equity, or place a creditworthy borrower in a lower credit-rated (and more expensive) loan, all to the benefit of the lender."[3]

> **When you do things God's Way, He will always provide. You can ask Him to open up opportunities for you, to provide for you, and He will.**

"Deceptive" is the word that God uses to describe Satan, so this should give us a clue that this is not God's Way. If you can trust God, you will wait for Him to give you the help you need. Proverbs 3:5 tells us, "Trust in the Lord with all your heart and lean not on your own understanding." God wants to be involved in every part of your life, including your business. Proverbs 3:6 reassures us, "In all your ways acknowledge Him, And He shall direct your paths."

Ask God About Your Plans

When I am considering a loan, I always ask God, "Lord, is this something that You think will be beneficial to my business? Or do you want me to wait on You to deliver?" I need to know that it is worth it because sometimes God tells me that even taking on $600 a month isn't what

---

3. Hayes, Adam, and Khadija Khartit. "Predatory Lending." Investopedia, IAC/Dotdash Meredith, February 18, 2022, investopedia.com/terms/p/predatory_lending.asp.

I am meant to do. Sometimes He has other plans for me that don't involve taking on good debt. And since I can't get good debt with a low credit score, I also know that God wants me to keep my credit score healthy.

When I took out the predatory working capital loan, I wasn't thinking, "What does God want me to do?" I didn't consider that I should wait on Him to manifest wealth for me. I was trying to fix everything on my own, and I didn't include God in my plans. By doing that, I was putting myself, my business, and my family in jeopardy.

Everything has to be done God's Way. When you try to take control and do it your way, you are putting yourself in a bad situation. Think about it like this — God would never want any of His people to be forced into a situation of usury with no room to breathe. The Lord would never want you to be held in financial bondage with no way to make your money back — only Satan does that.

Hold Yourself to a Higher Standard

You might ask, why? Why is it such a bad idea to get a predatory loan, if you are reasonably certain that you will be able to pay it off? As Kingdom business owners, we cannot put ourselves in that kind of financial situation. We must stay away from worldly schemes that entrap us because that state of bondage leads to demoralization and defeat. We become emotionally, physically, and spiritually depressed. This takes us away from preaching the Good Word, and it opens us up to Satan's designs.

You have a responsibility as a Kingdom person to spread the word of God. If you are being weighed down by an albatross around your neck, you can't do that effectively. God doesn't want Kingdom people operating from that state of overwhelm and lack.

As my dad used to say, "Remember, if it sounds too good to be true, it probably is." If your bank tells you that you can't even get a $5,000 loan, but a working capital loan company wants to give you $50,000, take that for what it is — it is Satan tempting you. When you don't keep your credit score high, it opens you up to whatever Satan has for you. His ultimate goal is to steal, kill, and destroy. If he can do that in one blow, he will.

Good Credit Matters

In life and in business, good credit matters. We should do everything we can to pay our bills on time. Paying our bills in a timely manner keeps us from having to yield to high interest rates and submit to Satan's schemes. Bad credit or slow credit can eat into our profits. God wants us to live in overflow, and paying high interest loans for business, cars, or homes can rob us of our future savings and retirement funds. The more we give away, the less we have for ourselves and for the Kingdom. Our credit is a representation of who we are. It lets the world know whether we have patience, it shows whether we trust in God, it indicates whether we're content, and it reveals whether our financial decisions are wise or foolish.

In the United States, you can go to school for twelve years and never be educated on accounting, credit, or credit reports. It is not your fault if you didn't receive this education, but it is still your responsibility to learn. This deficiency in our schooling stems from spiritual wickedness. The Bible says in Ephesians 6:12, "For we wrestle not against flesh and blood, but against principalities, against powers, against the rulers of the darkness of this world, against spiritual wickedness in high places." Do you think it's a coincidence that our children are not being taught the importance of credit? No, it is a satanic strategy designed to rob the ignorant.

It is our duty as Kingdom people to learn all that we can about managing our finances so that we and the Kingdom may prosper. The Lord says, "For I know the plans I have for you, plans to prosper you and not to harm you, plans to give you hope and a future." (Jeremiah 29:11)

When You Borrow, Always Repay

Our credit as a borrower tells a lender how well we budget and manage money. It shows if we're stretching ourselves too thin, and it indicates whether we're trustworthy. Several years back, I was behind on my tire account with one of my suppliers. I was having a truly difficult season in my business. At the time, I had more bills than money from overextending myself. My supplier knew me to be a man of God. After waiting on my payment for several weeks, he emailed me a message along with my bill. His email message was a scripture from Psalm 37:21: "The wicked man borrows and does not repay, but the righteous man shows mercy and gives." I was mortified. I felt awful. I cried out to

God to increase my income so I could pay off my debt. God soon blessed me with some extra sales, and the first thing I did with this money was to repay my supplier. The lesson to be learned is this: please educate yourself on credit and debt, and make sure to keep a careful budget so that you can track every dime that you spend. This will allow you to preserve your good name and keep your business in good standing.

I know firsthand how important credit is. I even took classes and became a credit repair specialist. My high school never taught me about credit, but that is no excuse for ignorance. I have taken on the responsibility to educate myself so that I'm not being robbed of my prosperity.

Safeguard Your Good Name

I have learned of the importance of protecting your good name. For example, your credit score is your good name as a business owner. So, don't tarnish it by spending more than you can afford. As my tire supplier reminded me in quoting Psalm 37:21, "The wicked borrow and do not repay, but the righteous give generously."

Before I learned about credit repair, there were times in my business when my credit score was low. I knew that it was a longshot to ask for bank loans based on my credit report, but I still had to try. I prayed to God and showed him that my heart was good, even if my credit was poor. As the Scriptures tell us in 1 Samuel 16:7, "Man looks at the outward appearance, but the Lord looks at the heart." God looked at my heart, and He allowed my

2 CORINTHIANS 9:6

But this I say: He who sows sparingly will also reap sparingly, and he who sows bountifully will also reap bountifully.

COLOSSIANS 2:8

Beware lest anyone cheat you through philosophy and empty deceit, according to the tradition of men, according to the basic principles of the world, and not according to Christ.

LUKE 16:10-11

Whoever can be trusted with very little can also be trusted with much, and whoever is dishonest with very little will also be dishonest with much. So if you have not been trustworthy in handling worldly wealth, who will trust you with true riches?

loan officer to give me the opportunity I needed. When God opens a door for you, do everything to represent Him well. I did this by repaying the bank in a timely manner and honoring my word with my loan officer.

Loans are an important vehicle for growing your business. They put you in a good position for receiving investment opportunities, and they allow you to purchase inventory and equipment that will get you to the next level. There will be a time in your business when you're going to need credit, and let me remind you, good credit matters! Good credit matters in business as it does in life. Now, you may have heard some people say, "Loans are just debt, and all debt is bad." While it is true that loans are debt, let me remind you that there are two types of debt — good debt and bad debt. You're able to access good debt when you've properly planned your business, you've studied the market, you know the pros

> **God would never want any of His people to be forced into a situation of usury with no room to breathe.**

and cons of your industry, and you are using your loan to make an investment in your business. Good debt allows you to take what you have borrowed and earn a good return on your investment. Even though the bank is charging you interest, your business can make so much profit during this timeframe that these costs are offset.

There will be times when you won't be approved for loans that would benefit your business. This is often due to having poor credit. In these situations, you are going to need God's help to sustain your business. Pray to God and ask Him to provide you His favor.

After I filed for bankruptcy, I worked hard to keep my business open. I went to several different warehouses and distribution centers, and I tried to purchase inventory so that I wouldn't have to drain my bank account every week. Unfortunately, nobody would approve me. Every time banks or other creditors said "no," I realized just how important good credit is.

The moral of this story is pay your bills on time and don't take on more debt than you can pay back within the loan period. Having good credit can be a matter of life and death for your business. In the Bible, it says, "A good name is to be chosen rather than great riches, and loving favor rather than silver and gold." (Proverbs 22:1) I tarnished my good name by overspending. I couldn't save my business, but God could. I prayed to Him as my business partner, and He showed me His forgiveness. He allowed my business to survive so that I could continue to serve His Kingdom. When you mess up your credit and your good name, you've got to rely on God to see you through. God provided for me, and He will provide for you too.

Bear Witness to God's Miracles

I'll never forget, back when I was struggling, I went and purchased some tires from a gentleman in my area who owns twelve tire stores. Within one month of our business relationship, he opened a line of credit for me. He said to me, "Whatever it is that you want, you let me know." He went even further. He gave me a key to his store near me and said, "Any time you get a service call at night when my store is close and you need a tire, you come here and get whatever you need."

I didn't even ask him for this credit line, nor a key to his store. God had put it in his heart to offer me these things. Thanks to God, I got the credit line that I so desperately needed.

God is the difference maker. When you don't have the credit, you better have a relationship with God. He will forgive you when you falter. Soon, my business began to flourish. The tire dealer saw that my business was doing well, and he allowed his salesmen to call me and ask, "Hey, Winston, is there anything we don't have at the shop that you need us to order for you?" This was a favor from God. I let them know that I needed semi tires. The tire dealer didn't do semi tires, but he put them in his inventory to help my business. When your credit is bad, but your God is good, you're in good hands. So, don't give up on your business. God will give you favor and allow the right people to show up as a blessing to you. God will extend a line of credit to you, even when man says you don't deserve it.

Everything You Need to Know About Business Is in the Bible

The Bible is free education. Truly, everything we need to know about business is laid out in scripture. Education is very important; however, you don't need an MBA to run a business. Even if you didn't go to college, the Bible gives you everything you require to be successful as a business owner. Hebrews 4:12 tells us, "For the

Word of God is quick and powerful, and sharper than any two-edged sword, piercing even to the division of soul and spirit, and of joints and marrow, and is a discerner of the thoughts and intents of the heart." If you study the Word, it's all right there: "But I would not have you to be ignorant, brethren." (1 Thessalonians 4:13)

Moreover, just as you should shun predatory loans, you should also beware of academic debt. If you choose to go to college, you must do it in an intelligent and purposeful manner. Avoid taking out large student loans, since academic debt will affect every aspect of your life for decades to come. Proverbs 22:7 tells us, "The rich rule over the poor, and the borrower is slave to the lender." You cannot afford to graduate saddled with hundreds of thousands of dollars in student loans and expect to get a job, let alone run a business. Even if you pick a "good major" (such as business, accounting, medicine, or law), having academic debt will still cripple you when you enter the workforce.

Every year, there are millions of dollars in academic grants and scholarships available to qualified students. If you are already in the workforce, there are work programs that will pay for you to go to college or technical school. Be smart in the way that you fund your education and don't take out excessive loans that you won't be able to pay back.

It's also important to address the opportunity cost of going to college. Every year that you spend in college is a year that you won't earn a full-time income. In this way, every college year costs you a full-time salary. If you graduate with student loans on top of this wage loss, you are doubly in debt.

I recommend to entrepreneurs and business owners that you get the amount of college education that you need to be successful, and then set out on your own as soon as you can. In Luke 14:28–30, Jesus said, "Which of you, wishing to build a tower, does not first sit down and count the cost to see if he has the resources to complete it? Otherwise, if he lays the foundation and is unable to finish the work, everyone who sees it will ridicule him, saying, 'This man could not finish what he started to build'."

Learn to Be Content

So, why is it that we accrue so much debt? What drives us to spend more than we can reasonably repay? Consumer debt is the result of being dissatisfied with what God has blessed us with. We all have a tendency to want to rush ahead of God. We want to force things our way, instead of doing things God's Way. Whenever we get out of alignment with God, it puts us in a bad situation.

If I had been content, I would not have gone into so much bad debt. I was trying to grow too fast in my business. I worked round the clock, getting up in the middle of the night, doing service calls at all hours, all to make someone else $30,000 in interest. I did all the work, and I gave them the money.

God's desire is for you to be happy, which is why Satan tries to destroy your peace of mind. When you get into debt, it drains you, financially, emotionally, mentally, physically, and spiritually. It squeezes the life out of you.

We all want to get rich quick, but this puts us against God. Hebrews 13:5 says, "Keep your lives free from the love of money and be content with what you have, for God has said: 'Never will I leave you, never will I forsake you'." The desire for quick cash puts us against our morals, like that one time in my business when I bought stolen tires. I was trying to do things in a hurry, climbing the ladder too fast, instead of doing things on God's time. My stress didn't just hurt me; it also affected my family. My wife and kids would wonder why I was so tired and overwhelmed all the time.

Since you are a Kingdom person, Satan will try to cheat you out of your money. As a business owner, you are a trailblazer. Loan officers have profiled you, and they know that you take risks. They also know if you have bad credit and if you have been denied a conventional business loan. They have everything at their disposal. Their ultimate goal is to make you work for them.

We must stay away from worldly schemes that entrap us because that state of bondage leads to demoralization and defeat

I don't want you to work hard, only for Satan to trick you out of what you have rightfully earned. I want you to work for your money, and for it to be a blessing to you. Know that what God has given you is enough. Don't live in a state of lack that makes you want to accumulate more and more. Be satisfied with what God is giving you right now, and don't try to grab from the future. Have the personal responsibility to pray to God and ask for His abundance. Trust in Him and know that He wants you to prosper: "I pray that you may prosper in all things and be in health, just as your soul prospers." (3 John 1:2)

When I was in financial bondage, I was so broken. I asked God, "Lord, I'm living righteously, I'm trying to do what's right, so why am I still struggling so much financially?"

God said to me, "Because you're not content. You keep putting yourself into bad financial

PROVERBS 30:24-28

There are four things which are little on the earth, but they are exceedingly wise: The ants are a people not strong, yet they prepare their food in the summer. The rock badgers are a feeble folk, yet they make their homes in the crags. The locusts have no king, yet they all advance in ranks. The spider skillfully grasps with its hands, and it is in kings' palaces.

situations that do not befit you as a Kingdom man. And now I have to pull you out of the hole you keep digging for yourself. Instead of filling your pockets, you are making me give your wealth to other people. Wait on Me. Trust in Me. Don't keep putting yourself deeper into debt that only benefits the thief."

Nowadays, I pray to God, and I say, "God, I'm satisfied with where You have me right now. I'm not going to get myself into a bad situation. I'm content until You open up another door for me. I'm going to wait for You to tell me what my next move should be."

Trust in God's mercy. Wait for Him to manifest His miracles in your life. He wants Kingdom people to survive and flourish. Even if you didn't trust Him before, He will still come to your aid. He will provide for you. When you make a bad investment, the average business partner will tell you that you're on your own. But not God. God gives us so much grace and provides us so much mercy: "The Lord is not slow in keeping his promise, as some understand slowness. Instead, He is patient with you, not wanting anyone to perish, but everyone to come to repentance." (2 Peter 3:9)

Don't Let Satan Tempt You

Debt causes you to be dishonest in your business. Sometimes, it makes you charge people more than you should; other times, it makes you take offers from customers that are lower than you should accept. You will do whatever you need to make your daily payments. When you are stuck in a bad financial situation, it feels like some money is better than no money at all.

Kingdom people can't put ourselves into a position that allows Satan to tempt us. He'll try to tempt us every day, but we can't take the bait. The Bible says that Satan even tried to tempt Jesus. He told Jesus, "If you are the Son of God, tell these stones to become bread." (Matthew 4:3) But Jesus said, "Man shall not live by bread alone, but by every word that comes from the mouth of God." (Matthew 4:4)

Satan will always try to lure us into bad contracts. We can't stop him from doing that. But what we can do is choose not to sign those deals with him. In Matthew 4:8–10, every time Satan tried to tempt Jesus, Jesus said no. He told Satan that it wasn't what God would want Him to do. Jesus never took Satan's bait:

MATTHEW 4:8–10

The devil took Him to a very high mountain and showed Him all the kingdoms of the world and their splendor.

"All this I will give you," he said, "if you will bow down and worship me."

Jesus said to him, "Away from me, Satan! For it is written: 'Worship the Lord your God, and serve him only'."

As Kingdom people, we need to be able to say no, even when Satan is tempting us with all the riches in the world. We need to be just like Jesus and recognize when something isn't what God wants for us.

I have learned from my mistakes, and I know that I have to follow the path that God has for me. When I go out into the community, I'll often see someone who is having a really hard day. What they need in that moment is a word from God through me. But if I'm stressed out and overwhelmed, I can't help anyone else. I am no good to anyone in my community if my mind is fixated on my debt. Since I'm human, I might just say to myself, "I've got my own problems. Why should I help someone else? Why should I spend time preaching the word of God if I have my own issues to worry about?"

At one point, I was so deep in debt that people would invite me to preach at their church, and I would turn down the opportunity because I had to work to repay my loans. I felt like it was just too high of a financial risk to take any time off from my job.

Whenever you put yourself into a position where you have to choose between what God wants you to do and what man wants you to do, you know you are in a bad situation. Every day that I wake up and my feet hit the ground, my focus should be on whatever God wants. As a Kingdom man, if I have to choose worldly matters over God, I know Satan is trying to get his hooks into me. Satan targeted me based on my Kingdom responsibilities. He knows that I am a Pastor, and so he put me in a situation where I couldn't preach the Gospel. Satan closed my mouth. I might as well have signed my soul over to the devil. Not only was it bad for my business and my family, but it was also bad for the Kingdom.

Renounce the Forbidden Fruit

God knows exactly what predatory loans are designed to do. From the beginning of time, God said to Adam, "You are free to eat from any tree in the garden; but you must not eat from the tree of the knowledge of good and evil, for when you eat from it you will surely die." (Genesis 2:16–17)

Then Satan came to Eve as the snake and tempted her with the fruit. He told her if she ate of the tree of knowledge, "You will not surely die." (Genesis 3:4)

In the same way, loan officers come to you and tell you, "This is a good deal! In fact, you can't beat this deal! You can't get a loan from anywhere else. This loan is not that horrible. Listen, I'm about to deposit $50,000 in your account tomorrow. It's not going to kill you."

Satan will take every opportunity to get in your ear. If you talk to him for long enough, he will deceive you. Eve allowed Satan to get in her ear, and that's how he was able to trick her into eating the forbidden fruit. He is a liar — don't listen to him. I've learned now what to do when the loan officers call me: I hang up the phone.

> **It is our duty as Kingdom people to learn all that we can about managing our finances so that we and the Kingdom may prosper.**

When you read the Bible, you will see that God has told us to stay away from these kinds of schemes. God could have made all the trees in the Garden available for Adam and Eve to eat. He has the power. Instead, He made one tree forbidden. In this way, He was letting Adam and

PHILIPPIANS 4:11

Not that I speak in regard to need, for I have learned in whatever state I am, to be content.

Eve know that He wasn't going to make them do the right thing; instead, He was going to give them a choice. There are many financial opportunities out there to help your business grow. It is your responsibility to refuse to partake in forbidden fruit that will end in death.

Trust in God's Design

God has already shown us what to do and what not to do, just as He did for Adam and Eve. When I made poor financial choices, I was always shameful before God. I felt bad about it because I knew that I'd done something that didn't line up with God's Word.

I want you to understand that Satan has no new tricks. He uses the same old schemes that he's used from the beginning. Now, he stays current with the times, and he dresses up his deceptions in a shiny new package, but underneath, it's the same strategy that he's used since he tempted Eve in the Garden. The Lord gives us a choice, and it's our responsibility to choose Him. When we do, God will bless us with abundance in ways that we can't even imagine.

Don't Ask God to Reward Poor Choices

What I understand now is that God is not responsible for our irresponsibility. He doesn't reward our bad financial choices. God wants us to make good decisions, but he also gives us Free Will. When Adam and Eve lived in the Garden, they knew exactly what they should and shouldn't do. They were not ignorant. God had already told them which trees they could eat from, and yet they chose the one that was forbidden.

I remember one day several years ago, I was sitting in a Waffle House reading my Bible. One of the waitresses came up to me and asked me what my purpose was for reading the Bible so openly. I explained, "I read the Bible so I can live according to God's Words. I want to understand God's Ways for my life, and I want to increase my faith in Him and know the direction He has for me so I can be blessed."

"Okay," said the waitress. "Well, I guess you should know that I'm an atheist. I don't believe in God."

"Really?" I asked her. "Why don't you believe in God?"

"Because my mom is a Christian," she said, "but I don't see God blessing her at all in return for her worship. My mom pays her tithes, but then she's always coming to me to ask for money."

I kept talking to the waitress to find out what else her mom did with her money. She told me, "Well, my mom gambles a lot. She's always playing the slot machines and the lottery, trying to win her way out of debt."

"I want to share something with you," I said. "This may change the way you feel about God. It may also help your mom see her finances in a new light. It's not God's fault when we make poor choices with our money. Even though your mom pays her 10% tithes, God still wants her to be responsible with the remaining 90%. He doesn't want her to make costly decisions, and He's not going to reward her for gambling or playing the lotto. Gambling and the lottery belong to Satan, not to God. That's why so many lotto winners are more unhappy after they win than they were before."

This waitress wanted a better life for her mom, but somehow, she thought that God would reward her mom for being a spendthrift. God doesn't want us to partake in get rich quick schemes, and we mustn't blame Him if we lose money. It is up to us to be frugal with the resources that He gives us. God shows us signs that we are headed in the wrong direction, but many times we choose not to listen. The waitress's mother was given plenty of signs that she was on the wrong path — losing money each week from gambling and playing the lotto — but she chose to ignore them.

> When God opens a door for you, do everything to represent Him well. I did this by repaying the bank in a timely manner and honoring my word with my loan officer.

Perhaps you know someone in the Kingdom like this, who tithes their 10%, but then waists the other 90% on frivolous things. Then they wonder why God doesn't give them everything they want, since they've tithed. But God isn't going to reward them for acting in a careless manner. He is going to reward them when they tithe their 10% *and* use the other 90% responsibly.

Moreover, I don't believe that this waitress was really an atheist; I think she was just someone who was angry with God. Many atheists are like this. They actually do believe in God, but they are mad at Him, so they turn away from Him like an indignant child does from a parent. Perhaps they or someone close to them have experienced a setback or a tragedy in their life, and they wonder why God has forsaken them. Remember that even Jesus had a moment of doubt. During his Passion on the Cross, he called out, "My God, My God, why have You forsaken Me?" (Matthew 27:46) Then He realized that it was all part of God's plan. God has a plan for everyone, but it may not be apparent in the moment.

I used to be a gambler in my younger life. I know firsthand what it feels like to work all week and then throw your money away, gambling up your paycheck. My gambling addiction lasted more than fifteen years, and I lost every dime that I made. We must all be conscious of Satan's schemes to attack our finances. I didn't start winning until God loosed me from the hands of the enemy. I finally quit gambling with no more desire to play. God delivered me from my addiction. I pray and bind every stronghold and addiction that inflicts you. Any stronghold that's hindering your finances through gambling, whether it's cards, slot machines, state lotto, or anything else. I bind the hands of the enemy right now over your life, and I loose deliverance in Jesus Mighty Name.

As a Kingdom man, if I have to choose worldly matters over God, I know Satan is trying to get his hooks into me.

Financial addictions happen when you're not content, and no matter how much money you have, it never feels like it's enough. Here is the solution: When you make money God's Way, you don't have to stay up all night playing cards like I used to do, hoping to win. When you're on God's team, you are already a winner.

Move from Poverty to Prosperity

God's ultimate goal is for us to live in prosperity, but because of disobedience and poor choices, we can go from living in Heaven to living in hell. As Kingdom people, we have a responsibility for being a light to the world. To do this, we must be obedient to God. We have a duty to ask, "What does God want me to do?"

A few years ago, I was asked to give a sermon at a church that was about 130 miles from my hometown. I accepted the engagement, and I drove down to preach the Word of God. A few days after I returned home, the preacher of the congregation called me up to express his gratitude. He told me something that made me realize just how important my work as a Kingdom person really is.

He said, "Pastor Grier, I want you to know that God really used you in a mighty way. Two people came to my office at church after your sermon, and they told me that they had been thinking about committing suicide. But your message helped them. God used you to raise them to the light."

Can you imagine if I had been in some bad debt, and I hadn't been able to take that trip? Just think about what would have happened if I had allowed Satan to put me in a bad financial situation where I wasn't able to take that assignment.

When you are so drained by debt, you can't answer to God's calling. You can't do what God wants you to do. When you can't move and go where God wants you to go, you can best believe that Satan is winning.

If I had not gone to that church to preach, two people might have taken their lives. But because I was there that day, God spoke through me, and He reminded them of His love for them. I was grateful to God that He allowed me to share something with someone that saved their life. That's why Satan wants us in debt and poverty. That's why he wants us operating from a place of lack. He doesn't want us blessing people and teaching them about what God can do.

I believe that suicidal thinking happens when people have lost hope and have reached a place where they don't feel that God can deliver them. They feel like there is no more help for them. If you are in that place, I want you to know that I've been there too. I know where you are. There is still help. God will still lift you up, like He lifted me up. God blessed me with abundance and overflow, and He will bless you too. There is hope for your business. No matter the mistakes you may have made in the past, there is hope for you because you have partnered with God. Starting from today, you've just got to do things God's Way.

that God is not responsible for our irresponsibility. He doesn't reward our bad financial choices. God wants us to make good decisions, but he also gives us Free Will.

Pastor Grier's Prosperity Prayer for Your Business

Dear kind and heavenly Father, I come to You as humble as I know how. God, I bind any spirit of debt, generational curses, and financial bondage, and I loose increase, overflow, and favor. Lord, I know Satan wants to attack my finances and my profits. Still, I'm not worried because You have power over the enemy. I ask right now that You break the hands of the enemy over my business and my personal finances, so that I can live an abundant life in Jesus' name.

Amen.

5

FOR WE ARE LABORERS TOGETHER WITH GOD

CHAPTER 5

For We Are Laborers Together with God

Building a Kingdom-Driven Team

In order to survive in business, you must surround yourself with an abundance of wisdom. Know what your services and products are worth, hire knowledgeable employees, and monitor your company's strengths and weaknesses. Above all, take time to educate yourself about the ideal customers that you wish to serve.

When you start your company, make sure you're strategically choosing the right people to be a part of your team. During my early years in business, one of the worst mistakes I made was hiring people that weren't able to elevate me. I know firsthand that this can be a matter of life or death for your business. Don't hire people because they're your friends or family. Don't hire them because you went to high school together or attend the same church. Hire a qualified team that has your best interests at heart. Every one of your employees should bring a level of knowledge and expertise to the table; only bring them on board if they enhance your company and your mission.

Let me remind you that Jesus carefully chose His disciples. Eleven of His apostles were honorable and blessed. There was only one unworthy disciple, and yet that was the man who betrayed Him. One bad apple out of twelve might not sound like terrible odds; however, one wrong decision can be a matter of life or death for your business as it was for Christ.

Building a team that can help your business grow is not only a smart business decision — it is a Kingdom decision. It is your responsibility to recruit workers who will help your business to flourish so you can contribute to the Kingdom. Proverbs 27:23 tells us, "Be sure you know the condition of your flocks, and give careful attention to your herds." In other words, make sure that you know at all times what's going on within your business.

Strengthen the Health of Your Business

Over the years, my uncle has given me many important pieces of business advice. One of his favorite sayings is, "I'm not going to pay someone to run my blood pressure up." What he meant by this was that we should hire employees that will reduce stress and make our businesses easier to run. Why is this important? Because if the health of your business is suffering, it will have a negative effect on the Kingdom. If you care about the Kingdom, you should care about your business affairs.

We must build our team with intention. As my uncle likes to say, "It's expensive to hire the wrong team."

Here are some of the positions that I recommend for your team:

- An employee who will be a praying warrior to intercede for you and your business.
- An employee with years or even decades of industry experience.
- An employee with formal education in your industry (this person can be a recent college graduate).
- An accountant with financial wisdom.
- A marketing expert with advertising experience.

Most of all, your team must consist of people who want to see your company make money God's Way, and they need to be able to level up as your business grows in its success.

Building a Kingdom-Driven Customer Base

Know the value of your company. As a Kingdom business owner, you must not sell yourself short or devalue your business because certain customers don't value your services or products. On the flipside, you mustn't behave in greedy or crooked ways just to get money quickly. There's nothing wrong with making money, but taking

ECCLESIASTES 4:9-10

Two are better than one, because they have a good reward for their labor. For if they fall, one will lift up his companion. But woe to him who is alone when he falls, for he has no one to help him up.

PROVERBS 13:20

He who walks with wise men will be wise, but the companion of fools will be destroyed.

advantage of people for fast financial gain is not doing business God's Way.

In business, we must sow what we want to reap. We are not serving the Kingdom if we cheat people and then claim to be servants of the Most High. We must be fair, not Christian crooks. I know firsthand that people will try to take advantage of our business, but that doesn't give us the right to take advantage of them in return. We must always remember that God can take two fish and five loaves of bread and feed thousands. He can also take our small, honest business and turn it into the biggest franchise in the world. God will give us an increase, but He will not reward us for cheating our customers.

Wisdom also extends to your business associations. It is unwise to disobey God's Words to make a connection that doesn't benefit the Kingdom. For instance, it may benefit your business to give discounts, be a sponsor, or engage in reasonable negotiations, but choose wisely. It's important that you know to whom you belong and what you're contributing towards.

Before you invite another party to engage with your business, ask yourself these questions:

- Am I partnering with an organization that represents God?
- Am I making a wise decision for the Kingdom?
- Am I being a blessing to my community and my country?

Be Wise in Choosing Your Customers

Ask God for spiritual discernment to protect you from unforeseen danger from people who are sent to you by Satan. God will warn you about certain people. He will communicate to you that these people are not meant to be your customers. When God gives you these cautionary signals, He is helping you with your Kingdom business management.

Be on the lookout for customers who want something for nothing. They will test the God in you and push you to the limit. Remain patient, for this is only a test. I believe that a stingy customer is worse than no customer at all. If you have customers that don't allow you to earn a decent profit, then respectfully leave those customers alone — they are not sent to you by God. It is your duty as a Kingdom business owner to be vigilant of Satan's strategy to rob and destroy you financially. As one of my favorite teachers, L.O. Bacon, used to say, "There is a price tag for ignorance, and it is the devil who makes us pay."

Know what your services and products are worth, hire knowledgeable employees, and monitor your company's strengths and weaknesses. Above all, take time to educate yourself about the ideal customers that you wish to serve.

Not everyone is your ordained customer, and that is okay; you will not be able to satisfy everyone in your business. Pray to God to give you the wisdom and intelligence to separate the wheat from the chaff. God wants above all else for you to prosper, so you will be wise to deal only with

For we are laborers together with God; you are God's field, you are God's building. According to the grace of God which was given to me, as a wise master builder I have laid the foundation, and another builds on it. But let each one take heed how he builds on it. For no other foundation can anyone lay than that which is laid, which is Jesus Christ.

customers that are in alignment with God's Words. Pray to God and ask Him to show you who He wants you to serve in your business, and who He wishes you to refrain from helping. Trust that God will place customers in your path that will grow your business, elevate the Kingdom, and keep you free from harm.

Avoid Customers That Cost You Money

I'll never forget, I was sitting at my desk one afternoon, and through the front glass windows, I saw a gentleman getting ready to enter my shop. God immediately said to me, "Do not do business with that man." The man came to the front desk and told me what he needed. It turned out that he was requesting a relatively simple upgrade for his vehicle, and it was a service that my team provided. Plus, it seemed like it would be a nice financial win for my business. So, I put money over God, and I chose to ignore the warnings that the Lord was giving me. We did a great job for this gentleman, but an hour later he called and claimed that my guys had scratched up his rims. God immediately spoke to me and said, "Didn't I tell you to bypass him?" I knew we didn't mess up his rims because I had installed them myself. Then he demanded that I give him an outrageous amount of money to "fix" his rims. I asked him to bring the wheels to me so my rim company could handle any repairs, since they would do it for a much lower price. I called him twice to resolve this issue, but he never showed up. In fact, it's been eight years now. The reality was that he was lying about his rims;

he thought that I would accept his lies without proof and simply write him a check. Unfortunately, his grift didn't stop there. He went around telling people, several of whom I know, that my business had damaged his wheels. A few people believed him, but most who know me know better. I wish I had listened to God. It would have saved my name from being tarnished by the lies he told.

Recognize When Customers Are Not Meant for You

An important lesson of making money God's Way is that not all money is good money. Be wise and follow God's direction. There are people who will come to eat at your restaurant just to spread lies about your food and your service. There are people that will buy a car from you just to spread rumors that you sold them a lemon. Again, not all customers are for you. Satan will send in his team to tear your business down, but wisdom from God will protect you if you listen and obey Him. Remember, some customers cost you money. When God tells you to avoid a potential client, do as He commands, no matter what the world might say.

Here are some questions to ask yourself when a potential customer approaches you:

- Will this transaction help me win souls?
- Is this transaction important to the Kingdom?
- Is this deal in alignment with God's Word?

3 JOHN 1:8

Therefore we ought to support such men, so that we may be fellow workers for the truth.

ECCLESIASTES 7:12

For wisdom is a defense as money is a defense, but the excellence of knowledge is that wisdom gives life to those who have it.

PROVERBS 1:19

Such are the paths of all who go after ill-gotten gain; it takes away the life of those who get it.

- Will this customer bring prosperity or harm to my business?
- Is this customer trying to haggle down my prices below what I can offer?
- Will my accountant recommend this transaction or business decision?

We should always listen to our spiritual warnings and be mindful of what the Word of God promises us in Psalms 91:3–4: "Surely He shall deliver you from the snare of the fowler and from the perilous pestilence. He shall cover you with His feathers, and under His wings you shall take refuge; His truth shall be your shield and buckler."

It is God's desire that you prosper, for He doesn't want His Kingdom business owners to take a loss. When you lose in business, the Kingdom suffers, so you can rest assured that God is watching over you.

Be Mindful of Those Who Would Rob Your Business

In business, there is a time and a season for all things: "a time to get, and a time to lose; a time to keep, and a time to cast away." (Ecclesiastes 3:6) So, please be mindful of people who try to harm your company. When we allow people to cheat us out of our services or products, we're allowing them to strategically hinder our finances, our business, and the Kingdom.

Here is a story to illustrate this point. Two of my Mom's brothers are business owners. Both are shop owners and very talented construction workers. My Uncle Johnny asked my Uncle Will to assist him with some houses he would be remodeling for a real estate company. My Uncle

Will went to see the homes to assess their condition and give my Uncle Johnny a general estimate of his cost to help. My Uncle Johnny had already given the real estate company an estimate. This estimate was extremely low compared to the market rate.

My Uncle Will asked his brother, "Why are you charging them such a very low price?"

My Uncle Johnny replied, "Because the guy who owns the real estate company will loan me money when I need it."

Here is the wisdom I learned from my Uncles that day. My Uncle Will told his brother, "You should charge the man what you deserve. Give him a fair price without working for nothing, and you won't need him for a loan."

I will never forget this conversation. It made so much sense. This company was secretly getting everything they wanted, while paying little to nothing for it. My Uncle Johnny was working tirelessly and getting a loan in return, which equaled bad debt and bondage. This is proven in Proverbs 22:7: "The rich rule over the poor, and the borrower is slave to the lender." Don't let Satan rob you of your gifts, talents, services, or products. Know your worth!

Now, you may ask, how did this hurt the Kingdom if it was a matter that only concerned my Uncles? Consider this: If my Uncle Johnny does a job for only $100,000 when he should be charging $150,000, he's hindering the Kingdom. When he tithes his 10%, the Kingdom will get only $10,000 instead of the $15,000 it de-serves. This one instance may look like it's only a $5,000 loss, but if Satan robs thousands of

> **God will warn you about certain people. He will communicate to you that these people are not meant to be your customers.**

PROVERBS 4:7

Wisdom is the principal thing; therefore get wisdom. And in all your getting, get understanding.

PROVERBS 1:33

Whoever listens to Me will dwell safely, and will be secure, without fear of evil.

PROVERBS 3:35

The wise shall inherit glory, but shame shall be the legacy of fools.

Kingdom businessmen and women in this way, it will all add up. Satan's ultimate goal is to destroy the Kingdom, and he doesn't care if he starts with finances. The best way to ruin a business partnership is when one of the partners is not getting his true percentage of the agreement. Don't let man rob your business partner. God's wisdom and the Holy Spirit will always expose Satan's evil intent and protect your business. God is watchful of thieving customers who hinder the Kingdom by working you for pennies.

Be a Blessing to Customers in Need

Never let people take advantage of your business, but always help when God says so. Know that there may be times that God will tell you to do things as a business owner that do not make sense to you. Remember what Proverbs 3:5 tells us: "Trust in the Lord with all your heart, and lean not on your own understanding." Listen to God's wisdom and be not afraid, for He is guiding you on the path that He has set out for you. "My sheep hear My voice; I know them, and they follow Me." (John 10:27)

Build Goodwill in the Kingdom

I remember one day, a gentleman called me for roadside services. He was stranded and out of fuel. God spoke to me and said, "Give him a low price to assist him." I did as God commanded, but when I hung up the phone, I realized that the price I had just charged him seemed far too low to travel forty miles. I started to worry. Satan spoke in my ear and said, "Call him back and quote him a higher price." I shook my head. I knew that I couldn't change the price now, even though it was too low. I must be a man of my word. I drove out and helped the man. As we were talking, I found out that he was a tire wholesaler. God had told me to offer the low roadside service price in order to forge a connection for my business. Even though I didn't initially understand God's plan, I followed His commands.

God rewarded me for my obedience to Him. The next week, the man called and said his truck was coming to my area, and he asked if I wanted semi tires. I hesitated since I didn't have all the money I needed. I told him what I wished to buy, and I asked him to give me a few weeks to gather the funds. Instead of waiting, he decided to put together my order. He trusted me to come through. He delivered me a load of tires, telling me, "Pay whatever you can now, and then pay the balance once you sell them." He sent a truck to stock my shop, even though I didn't have enough money to pay the full bill.

Satan had tried to interfere by telling me to charge him more for the roadside call, but I knew that I must ignore the enemy. God awarded me with instant credit just because I had been obedient to Him. God allowed this man to find favor in me and trust me. To this day, he is still my tire supplier because I listened to God. God is my business partner, and I know that I must believe in Him and do what He says.

There is an abundance of gold and rubies, but lips of knowledge are a rare treasure.

The fear of the LORD is the beginning of knowledge, but fools despise wisdom and instruction.

The fear of the LORD is the beginning of wisdom, and the knowledge of the LORD is understanding.

Win Souls for the Kingdom

On another occasion, a truck driver called me with one blown out tire, but God told me to load two tires in my truck. I went out to help the driver, and I noticed he had another tire that was nearly as bad. I took him to the back of the trailer to show him how worn the other tire was. He looked at it sadly and said, "I only budgeted on fixing the one tire. I'm going to try to make it to my destination, so hopefully the other tire will hold." Then he got back in his truck while waiting for me to finish the job.

> **God is my business partner, and I know that I must believe in Him and do what He says.**

God spoke to me while I was replacing the tire. The Lord said, "Give him the second tire you loaded."

I was surprised. I said, "What is it you want me to do, God?"

He said it again, "Give the man the second tire."

I went to the front of the truck and knocked on the driver's door, showing him the second tire that I'd loaded. I told him, "You really need your other tire replaced. I'm going to give you this new tire."

As soon as I said this, the man's eyes welled up with tears. He said to me, "Now I know there's a God."

He explained to me how his trucking business had been a challenge for him all year. He was taking the load to Texas, and he knew that the tire wasn't going to make it. He said that when I'd told him about the other tire, he had started praying because he didn't have any more money to give me. He prayed that God would allow him to make it to Texas so he could get paid and pay his commercial insurance. While he was praying, God showed him mercy and told me to give him the other tire.

PROVERBS 3:13

Happy is the man who finds wisdom, and the man who gains understanding.

PHILIPPIANS 2:2

Fulfill my joy by being like-minded, having the same love, being of one accord, of one mind.

I had no idea the truck driver was praying to God, but God knew. God understood that the man needed the second tire even before he called me to fix his truck. That's how I know that my actions that day came from Divine inspiration. You see, whenever I'm dispatched for a semi tire replacement, I only take what the customer asks for. Semi tires are so heavy that carrying extras is impractical. But that day, God told me to take two. Even before the man started praying, God was already mindful of his situation. The Lord was concerned about the man's business and finances, and He was already using me to make a way for him. God knew that by helping this man, I would help secure his faith in the Almighty. My actions that day helped win a soul for the Kingdom.

Now, some of you may say, "That was very thoughtful of you, Pastor, but you took a loss." No, I didn't. For the rest of the day, God sent many more customers to me. I did more truck tires on that day than I had ever done on a single day before. I was so glad that I had listened to God. If God tells you to help someone, do it. Trust me, you're never losing when you obey the Lord, because He will repay you. He may not reimburse you immediately, but when He does, He will see to it that you receive tenfold what you have given. Remember, when you obey God, there is always a reward in heaven that man cannot give. Money is not the only way God can repay you. He can give you and your family good health and favor, just to name a few things. There are so many ways God can bless you.

Pastor Grier's Wisdom Prayer for Your Business

Dear kind and heavenly Father, I pray that You surround me with people that have wisdom and knowledge, but most importantly, people who give me understanding. Allow me to be led by Your Holy Spirit, submit to Your directions, and always follow Your path, even when I do not yet understand it. God, I trust You to provide me with the right team and the right customers that will heed Your words, be a blessing for the Kingdom, and be prosperous for my business. All these blessings I ask in Your Son Jesus' name.

Amen.

6

LOVE YOUR ENEMIES AND PRAY FOR THOSE WHO CURSE YOU

CHAPTER 6

Love Your Enemies and Pray for Those Who Curse You

Your Opposition Cannot Harm You

In life, there will always be people who don't want you to succeed. These people may be your competitors, your frenemies, or even your family. No matter what they try to do to destroy your business, be not afraid. They will not succeed. When you put your faith in God and align yourself with His Word, the Lord will make your enemies your footstool. Any time your enemies attempt to tear you down, God will ensure that they elevate you instead. Believe, trust, and obey the Lord, and He will protect your business from Satan's schemes.

A number of years ago, I was having some financial difficulties, and I was behind on my payments for my service truck. One day, the repo guy came to repossess my truck, which at the time was my only service vehicle. Before he took my truck, however, he knocked on my door, which is unusual for repo guys. They normally have a spare set of keys with them, so they just get in your vehicle and drive it away. Instead, this gentleman did me the courtesy of showing up on my doorstep. He said to me, "The bank sent me to come and repossess your truck. But I don't feel like taking it. I don't know why, but something tells me not to."

Glory. Hallelujah. This was God at work. You see, repo workers don't get paid by the hour; they get paid each time they bring back a car. Whenever they see a car to repossess, they know it's a payday for them, so they have an incentive to avoid the vehicle's owner. Their goal is to drive the vehicle away or tow it before anyone can stop them, and then they call the police to report it repossessed so the owner can't claim that their vehicle was stolen. When this repo man came to take my truck, God intervened. The man told me, "Here, take my card. Call me when you catch up on the payment. I'm the only one on the case, so no one else will be by." God had put it in the man's head and heart to be lenient to me, even though it meant that he was forfeiting his paycheck.

The next week, God sent me more than enough work, and I caught up with my payments. God was showing me that whatever may befall my business, it will not destroy me. He let me know, "I will make your enemy bless you." God allowed the repo man to be my friend. This was a Divine intercession because I know the man wanted to earn his commission. But instead of turning me in, he chose to save me.

God will always fight for Kingdom businessmen and women. When you obey the Lord, He will protect you. The hands of God are in your life, and God will remind you that His heart's desire is for you to prosper. Satan wants to stop your business from feeding your family and the Kingdom, but God will fight your battle. Continue to make money God's Way, and He will transform your enemies into your stepping stones to success.

Winning Against Your Opposition

Early in my career, I had a competitor who would always talk friendly with me in person but would badmouth my business to other people in order to increase his sales. I was mad when I found out that he was trash-talking me behind my back. Satan got in my ear and said, "Go get him straight," but God told me to stop. The Lord counseled me, "Leave the man be. Let Me sort him out." At the time, it was hard for me to bite my tongue, but I listened to God, and I stayed obedient to Him. A few months later, the man called me and said he was closing down and moving from Georgia to Florida. He sold me his equipment and all his tires for less than half price. God said to me, "You see? Had you opened your mouth, he never would have offered to sell you his inventory, let alone give it to you at a discount." This was a big aha moment for me. Do not let Satan tempt you into taking revenge. Instead, let God deal with your haters. When you do business God's Way, He will ensure that your opposition cannot touch you.

JEREMIAH 39:17-18

"But I will deliver you in that day," says the LORD, "and you shall not be given into the hand of the men of whom you are afraid. For I will surely deliver you, and you shall not fall by the sword; but your life shall be as a prize to you, because you have put your trust in Me."

PSALMS 110:1

The LORD said, "Sit at my right hand, until I make your enemies your footstool."

JOHN 16:33

"I have said these things to you, that in Me you may have peace. In the world you will have tribulation. But take heart; I have overcome the world."

Let God Send Strangers to Bless You

Throughout your years in business, you will have family members, friends, and associates that applaud you in public but secretly hope for your downfall. You may feel hurt by this, but you will get through it. These people are simply not meant to be your customers. During my fifteen years in business, I've had family and friends that have never come to me when they needed tires. Instead, they went to one of my competitors. Rather than getting angry about this, I give thanks to God that He has protected me from people who do not want to help my business flourish. I don't let their lack of patronage distract me because I know that God will always send strangers to bless me in their place.

> Satan wants to stop your business from feeding your family and the Kingdom, but God will fight your battle. Continue to make money God's Way, and He will transform your enemies into your stepping stones to success.

In Genesis 12:1–3, The Lord said to Abraham, "Go from your country, your people and your father's household to the land I will show you. I will make you into a great nation, and I will bless you; I will make your name great, and you will be a blessing. I will bless those who bless you, and whoever curses you I will curse; and all peoples on earth will be blessed through you." When you make money God's Way, He will send customers to you so that your business can prosper. He will send certain people to you that He wants you to help, but there will be others that He wants you to avoid. When a person in your family or your friend group is reluctant to do business with you, don't force them to. I guarantee you that no matter what you do to help them, they won't be satisfied. Release them, and it will be for your own good.

I've served more customers from out of state than I have in my local area. People traveling from all over the country break down near my city and call me to replace their tires. I'll never forget, God once sent a trucker from Texas to my tire shop. He was very happy with my service, and he made sure to put my number in his phone for when he next drove through Georgia. A few months later, he called me again. He had been on the road for several days, and he knew soon into his trip that he would need one of his tires replaced. It was nearly bald. He phoned me and said, "I'm on the way to Georgia from Texas and need some semi tires, but I don't know if I'm going to make it. I'm praying to God that I can reach your shop before my tire blows out. I'd much rather have you change my tires than have to find someone else." I told him to keep me posted, and that I would do everything I could to help him. He called me the next day and said, "I just had a blowout. I'm in Georgia, but I don't think I'm close enough for you to help me. Let me tell you where I am, and maybe you can recommend another shop."

When the man gave me his location, I knew that God had interceded for both of us. God had put him within twenty miles of my shop when his tire finally gave out, which was close enough for my roadside team to help him. We drove out to where he was, and we replaced his tires. How he made it that far on a bald tire was nothing short of a miracle. The man told me that he was so impressed by my used tire quality and my service that he would continue to do business with me again. Even

TITUS 2:7-8

Show yourself in all respects
to be a model of good
works, and in your teaching
show integrity, dignity, and
sound speech that cannot
be condemned, so that an
opponent may be put to
shame, having nothing evil to
say about us.

though he lived hundreds of miles away, he would always wait until he came to Georgia to purchase tires. This was humbling for me.

God told Abraham to leave his father's household and set out to a land that he had never seen before. The Lord promised that He would send strangers to him that would be a blessing. God did this for Abraham, and He will do this for you too. Even if people close to you refuse to frequent your business, do not let that defeat you. Forgive them, pray for them, and if it is within God's Plan, He will change their hearts. When you let these people go, God will send strangers to you to be a blessing. Trust that God has your back.

Forgive Those Who Are Filled with Envy

You will also have people in your life who are ruled by Satan. Their ultimate goal is to tear your business down. Satan has filled their hearts with jealousy, and they don't want to see you prosper. Forgive them, for they are choking every day on the poison of their own envy. No matter how hard they may try to hinder you from being blessed, neither fight them nor attempt to persuade them. Let them go. The only One you need on your team is God. He will send you customers to take the place of the people who won't patronize you.

The scriptures are true: "Where your treasure is, there will your heart be also." (Matthew 6:21) For example, if a friend of mine were in the peanut business, and I didn't eat peanuts, I would buy a pack for someone else to show my support and love for my friend's company. In other words, if someone wants you to succeed, there are many ways for them to contribute to your business.

Let me reassure you that God will make a way for you, regardless of your opposition. We serve the same God who opened doors for Abraham, and who parted the Red Sea for the children of Israel. We serve the same God who called Lazarus back to life after he had been in the grave for four days. As a Kingdom businessman or woman, you may think you're losing in the same way that Mary thought she had lost her brother Lazarus, but here is the truth — no devil in hell can stop the blessing and favor that God has for those of us who make money God's Way.

There will always be jealous people in your life that you will never be able to satisfy. They will pay your competition $15,000, but expect you to perform the same service for $5,000. In order for potential customers to do business with you, they must value three things: you, your products, and your services. Don't allow people to devalue you. Know your worth. When someone appreciates your products or services, they'll happily pay you what you deserve. Don't lower your standards to gain someone's approval who doesn't want to patronize you in the first place.

Avoid Those Who Sow Discord

I have a family member who owns a salon. She is well known for doing hair, so she was disappointed when one of her close friends wouldn't do business with her; instead, this woman chose to get her hair done by a competitor. One day, my family member

MALACHI 3:11

"And I will rebuke the devourer
for your sakes, so that he will not
destroy the fruit of your ground,
nor shall the vine fail to bear
fruit for you in the field," says the
LORD of hosts.

ROMANS 12:19

Beloved, do not take revenge, but
leave room for God's wrath, for it is
written: "Vengeance is Mine, I will
repay," says the LORD.

ISAIAH 54:17

"No weapon formed against
you shall prosper, and every
tongue which rises against you in
judgment you shall condemn. This
is the heritage of the servants of
the LORD, and their righteousness
is from Me," says the LORD.

decided to give her friend a birthday gift of a free hairstyle to earn her business; she did a great job, but she didn't get the results from her friend that she'd hoped for. Instead of showing gratitude, her friend rewarded her generosity by complaining to their mutual acquaintances about the hairstyle that she had gotten for free.

Let me be clear, there's nothing wrong with complaining when you're not satisfied. If you have a problem with a product or service that you've received, you should tell the business owner about your concerns. However, it is dishonest to spread lies about a business to try and sabotage them. It causes discord, and it can lead to defamation lawsuits. If you have a problem with my business, but you complain to others and not to me, then I know that your objective is to stir up confusion, not to solve problems. The Scriptures tell us that these motives are satanic and not Godly: "For God is not the author of confusion but of peace." (1 Corinthians 14:33) To put this in perspective, if I am disappointed with a purchase I made at Walmart, I wouldn't go to the Dollar General customer service department to complain. I would go back to the Walmart where I did business.

When customers sow discord instead of giving constructive criticism, know that they are sent by Satan to try and tear you down. Let these customers go, and do not try to appease them. God will deal with them in His Way. What God has intended for you is meant for you to have; what He doesn't intend for you is withheld for your good. God has customers waiting to bless your business. Direct your marketing and outreach to these people. They are ordained to you, and they are glad to sing your praises from the rooftops.

Dealing with Customers Who Cheat You

Earlier this year, I went out to install a new tire for a customer in Greensboro, Georgia. After I finished the installation, the customer told me that he didn't have enough money to pay me. He said that he would drive to a gas station ATM to get cash.

I followed behind him, but when he approached the exit to the gas station, he sped off down the interstate. I realized too late that it had been his intent all along to cheat me of what he owed me.

I called the police to report the theft, but State Patrol wasn't able to apprehend him. I tried to catch up to him, but God told me to slow down. He said, "Don't get yourself killed over a little money. Do not worry, for I will repay you."

> **We must always represent God and the Kingdom well, no matter how disrespectful a customer may be. When we are patient and kind to rude customers, our forgiveness shows them the goodness of God.**

The very next evening, a truck driver called me from the exact same location and asked me to bring him a couple of semi tires. He was pleased with my work and paid me in full. Then the evening after that, another truck driver called me from the same location, requesting three semi tires for his trailer. Rarely will a truck driver require three tires on one road call. He also paid me in full.

God was showing me His determination to restore me. He reminded me, "I told you that I will repay you. I have intentionally blessed you in the exact spot where Satan chose to rob you." God was reassuring me that Satan had not won.

2 THESSALONIANS 3:3

But the Lord is faithful, who will establish you and guard you from the evil one.

DEUTERONOMY 28:7

The LORD will cause your enemies who rise against you to be defeated before your face; they shall come out against you one way and flee before you seven ways.

ISAIAH 49:25

But thus says the LORD: "Even the captives of the mighty shall be taken away, and the prey of the terrible be delivered; for I will contend with him who contends with you, and I will save your children."

I want to encourage you not to give up. We live in a sinful world, and there will always be wicked people out there. But if you do business God's Way, you have nothing to worry about. God will multiply sales for you.

Dealing with Customers Who Are Rude to You

When you are in business, dealing with rude customers is inevitable. In 1 Peter 4:1, the Bible tells us, "Therefore, since Christ suffered for us in the flesh, arm yourselves also with the same mind, for he who has suffered in the flesh has ceased from sin." In other words, you will encounter harsh people just as Christ did. You may experience this incivility in person, over the phone, via email, or on social media. When this happens, remember the saying, "The customer is always right." Dealing with disrespect is a Kingdom test that you must pass.

When Christ was on the cross, he was spat on, pierced in his side, ridiculed, beaten, falsely accused, and called everything but a Child of God. Christ is our example. He passed the test and said, "Father, forgive them, for they know not what they do." (Luke 23:34)

We must always represent God and the Kingdom well, no matter how disrespectful a customer may be. When we are patient and kind to rude customers, our forgiveness shows them the goodness of God. It doesn't matter if the customer is wrong; we still must do as Christ would do and forgive those that persecute us.

We know this from Matthew 5:8–12: "Blessed are the pure in heart, for they shall see God. Blessed are the peacemakers, for they shall be called sons of God. Blessed are those who are persecuted for righteousness' sake, for theirs is the Kingdom of Heaven. Blessed are you when they revile and persecute you, and say all kinds of evil against you falsely for My sake. Rejoice and be exceedingly glad, for great is your reward in Heaven, for so they persecuted the prophets who were before you."

When I first started out in business, I wasn't very effective at dealing with rude customers. I didn't understand that helping these individuals was a Kingdom test. When customers gave me a bad attitude, I would refuse to offer my services, and sometimes I would get into heated arguments. I justified my actions by saying that these customers reaped what they sowed; if they wanted to be treated better, they should adopt a better attitude.

However, as I grew closer to God, I came to understand that the Lord was sending these people to me to test my ability to show up for the Kingdom. Most of these customers needed someone to talk to them, encourage them, pray for them, and sometimes just listen to them. The people I serve are usually stuck on the side of the road, having an unexpected breakdown. They are forced to spend money that they haven't budgeted. In fact, they are possibly having one of the worse days of their life. This was my Kingdom assignment, and I couldn't continue to avoid these customers or turn them away. God told me that it was my duty as a Christian to communicate with love and understanding, for love is the answer to all things. It softens the hearts of those in crisis and allows God to help them.

Satan wants us to respond rudely in kind to rude customers, but we must not take the devil's

ZECHARIAH 9:12

Return to the stronghold, you prisoners of hope. Even today I declare that I will restore double to you.

ISAIAH 59:19

So shall they fear The Name of the LORD from the west, and His glory from the rising of the sun; when the enemy comes in like a flood, The Spirit of the LORD will lift up a standard against him.

PROVERBS 16:7

When a man's ways please the LORD, He makes even his enemies to be at peace with him.

But I say to you, love your enemies, bless those who curse you, do good to those who hate you, and pray for those who spitefully use you and persecute you.

bait. Vengeance sows discord in the Kingdom, which is what Satan wants. When we instead show love and forgiveness, and "turn the other cheek," we build the Kingdom up. We show our customers just how good the Kingdom is, and we make it more likely for them to frequent our business and other Kingdom businesses in the future.

You see, when a customer comes to you in a negative state, it means that Satan has stolen their joy. Satan wants to use their bad day to hinder you financially. The devil will try to speak through you to chase that customer away. Then they will leave and tell everyone how rude you were to them. This gives Satan a double victory. He recruits someone who will badmouth your company, and he keeps them from spending their money at a Kingdom business.

As Kingdom people, we can't stoop down to Satan's level. We have to know the devil's tricks. When the devil goes low, we must go high. It is our responsibility to be both professional and Godly. We must learn to have humility. It can be hard to humble yourself when you are not at fault, but you cannot fight fire with fire. Humbling yourself doesn't mean letting disrespectful people walk all over you; it means that you are humbling yourself before God. You are choosing love over anger, and forgiveness over blame. The Bible tells us, "Pray for those who spitefully use you and persecute you." (Matthew 5:44)

Remember that you are in partnership with God. Your rules are God's rules. Even though you are in the world, you should not be of the world. "Do not be conformed to this world, but be transformed by the renewal of your mind, that by testing you may discern what is the will of God, what is good and acceptable and perfect." (Romans 12:2)

In this way, you must still show people kindness, even when you don't think that they've earned it. Humility illuminates the God in you. "Let your light so shine before men, that they may see your good works and glorify your Father in heaven." (Matthew 5:16) When you do this, the same customer who yelled at you will come in two weeks later with their head bowed in contrition. They will be ashamed of their behavior, they will likely seek your pardon, and they may even ask to attend services at your church. Do not hold a grudge, for grudges weigh heavily around your neck. A grudge is like a yoke that binds you to Satan. Show grace and mercy and let your compassion flow freely.

Remember that you are in partnership with God. Your rules are God's rules. Even though you are in the world, you should not be of the world.

As followers of Christ, we must be Christ-like in business. Christ forgave those who brutalized and killed him, so we can certainly forgive those who are impolite to us. By choosing forgiveness, we are being the "bigger man," just like Christ. This sets an example for rude customers and shows them how to be better in their own lives.

Pastor Grier's Intercessory Prayer for Your Business

Dear kind and heavenly Father, You know that Satan's job is to steal, kill, and destroy, and so You have come to intercede on our behalf that we may live in abundance. I bind anything that Satan has set out to destroy in my business, and my prayer is that You would enlarge our Kingdom territory and loose financial overflow. Lord, You said that whatever we bind on earth, You will bind in Heaven, and whatever we loose on earth, You will loose in Heaven. God, I pray that You would continue to prepare a table before me in the presence of my enemies. That way, those who wish to see me fail will know that no matter how much they try to tear Kingdom people down, there is no one greater than You. All these blessings I ask for in your son Jesus' name.

Amen.

7

WORK HEARTILY, AS
FOR THE LORD AND
NOT FOR MEN

CHAPTER 7

Work Heartily, as for the Lord and Not for Men

Downsizing Your Business

There are times as a business owner when you need to downsize your business and work for someone else to build up your finances. I want to tell you my story of one of these times.

A few years ago, I found that I was unable to compete with the tire prices offered by big-box retailers and online stores. I made the difficult choice to close my tire shop, and I started doing roadside service only. After a few months, I decided to apply for a salaried position to help me better support my family. It would allow me to make a decent living, and I could still run my roadside division at night.

After owning my own business for fifteen years, the idea of working for someone else was a bit daunting. I didn't know what to expect. I was so used to being the one at the top calling the shots.

There was a job that I had my eye on. It was a logistics manager position, and I recognized that it would utilize many of the skills that I had developed running my business. I prayed on this job, and God said that I would be hired for the position. But a week or so after I applied, I found out that they had hired someone else. The position had been filled by a young woman. She didn't have much work experience, but she did have a college degree, which I didn't have at the time.

I was discouraged that I hadn't been chosen for the position. I'd felt in my soul that God was going to bless me with that job, and yet I didn't get it. I started wondering what God's plan was for me.

Then about two weeks later, the supervisor called me and asked, "Winston, are you still interested in this job?"

I told him, "Yes, sir. Absolutely."

I was confused. I knew they had already hired somebody in the role. However, I came to find out that they fired the lady after about two weeks. She had a college degree, but she didn't have enough work experience, and it turned out that she wasn't a great fit for the position.

As for me, I had exactly the kind of experience that they wanted, but I didn't have a college degree. So, the supervisor talked the president into giving me another interview, based on my work experience alone. They interviewed me again, and I got hired soon after.

As soon as they offered me the job, I prayed to God and thanked Him for His goodness.

God told me, "Winston, I told you I would come through for you."

About a month later, one of the senior employees came to my office. She was a white lady. She said to me, "Winston, I was wondering if I could share something with you?"

I told her, "Yes, ma'am."

She said, "You know, you're the first African American who has ever been hired in a corporate position in our company since I've worked here, and I've been here for twenty-one years. I'm not telling you this because I want you to feel bad about the company. I'm just saying this to let you know that I'm happy, and we're happy to have you aboard."

I thanked her for welcoming me. I said, "I appreciate you telling me."

After she left, I shut my office door because I started to get really emotional. I knew God had opened up a door for me to get that position, but I hadn't realized that God had opened a door for me that He had never opened for anyone else. God allowed this lady to come into my office to tell me this because sometimes God wants to remind us that he's here for us. He's got our back.

Since then, the company has hired another African American employee as a management trainee. That was one of my goals. I told the Lord, I want to represent my community and my God so well that the company will hire more African American employees in corporate positions.

God showed me that regardless of what man requires, you just need to focus on what God can do. Man hired a lady that had a college degree. God hired a man that had nothing at all, save for years of hard work.

When God does things, he's not looking for the qualifications of man. In the Bible, the Lord sent Samuel to the house of Jesse to seek the future

MATTHEW 6:28-33

So why do you worry about clothing? Consider the lilies of the field, how they grow: they neither toil nor spin; and yet I say to you that even Solomon in all his glory was not arrayed like one of these. Now if God so clothes the grass of the field, which today grows, and tomorrow is cast into the oven, will He not much more clothe you, O you of little faith? Therefore do not worry, saying, "What shall we eat?" or "What shall we drink?" or "What shall we wear?" For after all these things do the Gentiles seek. For your heavenly Father knows that you need all these things. But seek first the Kingdom of God and His righteousness, and all these things shall be added to you.

PROVERBS 16:18

Pride goes before destruction, and a haughty spirit before a fall.

King of Israel among Jesse's sons. One by one, the sons of Jesse passed by Samuel, but God's anointed was not among them.

1 SAMUEL 6:7-13

The Lord said to Samuel, "Do not look at his appearance or at his physical stature, because I have refused him. For the Lord does not see as man sees; for man looks at the outward appearance, but the Lord looks at the heart." (1 Samuel 16:7)

And Samuel said to Jesse, "The Lord has not chosen these." And Samuel said to Jesse, "Are all the young men here?" Then he said, "There remains yet the youngest, and there he is, keeping the sheep."

And Samuel said to Jesse, "Send and bring him. For we will not sit down till he comes here." So he sent and brought him in. Now he was ruddy, with bright eyes, and good-looking. And the Lord said, "Arise, anoint him; for this is the one!" Then Samuel took the horn of oil and anointed him in the midst of his brothers; and the Spirit of the Lord came upon David from that day forward. (1 Samuel 16:11–13)

At the time that Samuel found David, he was just a shepherd boy. He had the heart of a king, but he didn't yet have the credentials. Still, God saw to it that David was anointed. Man looks at the outer appearance, but God judges the heart. God knew David's heart, even though he was just a humble shepherd. In the same way, I didn't have a college degree, but I did have the heart to do the job.

Now, if you've been working for yourself for many years, you may not have a resume that appeals to an employer. That was the situation I was facing. When I created my resume, the only thing I could put on it was my work experience serving my customers. I was concerned that I wouldn't be able to find anyone to vouch for me. I shouldn't have worried, for God had my back.

God put it in the mind of my supervisor to ask three different people about me. These were not people I had put on my resume. One of the men he asked owned the parts store that served my business. This man vouched for me. He said, "I know Winston. He's a good man. He comes in here often, and we have great conversations about God. We talk about God and church all the time." He and I had made a meaningful connection over our faith. I didn't know it at the time, but he and my supervisor played golf together.

Being an entrepreneur has a lot of ups and downs. There are good seasons and hard seasons, and sometimes you need to acknowledge the hard season and decide to get a job.

God allowed my supervisor to ask all the right people about me. He saw to it that these people upheld my good name. The Scriptures tell us, "A man's heart plans his way, but the Lord directs his steps." (Proverbs 16:9) Trust God to order your steps. He knows exactly what He is doing, and He does everything right.

After I found this out, my wife said to me, "What if your supervisor had asked someone who didn't like you?"

JAMES 4:10

Humble yourselves in the sight of the Lord, and He shall lift you up.

JEREMIAH 29:11

For I know the plans I have for you," declares the LORD, "plans to prosper you and not to harm you, plans to give you hope and a future.

COLOSSIANS 3:23–24

Whatever you do, work heartily, as for the LORD and not for men, knowing that from the LORD you will receive the inheritance as your reward. You are serving the Lord Christ.

WINSTON GRIER

I said, "No, God doesn't work that way. God made sure that my supervisor found people who could vouch for me."

Downsizing has been a blessing. I am thankful to be able to work for myself while also having the stability of a 9 to 5. Being an entrepreneur has a lot of ups and downs. There are good seasons and hard seasons, and sometimes you need to acknowledge the hard season and decide to get a job.

Another benefit that I've gotten from my job is college tuition remission. I have started a college program for marketing management. My job includes tuition reimbursement. It gives me an opportunity to get a college degree without being weighed down by tens of thousands of dollars in academic debt.

Don't look at downsizing and getting a job as a bad thing. Use it in the way that God intends for you and make the best of it. Your business experience will ultimately make you a better employee. Running your own business gives you valuable leadership experience, which makes you an asset to any company you work for. I learned respect from being a boss, and I bring that integrity with me to my workplace.

Honoring the Season of Your Business

Downsizing means decreasing employees to decrease cost, which can be vital for your business. One of my biggest mistakes early on in my business was keeping several employees too long when I should have released them a year before. Downsizing at that time would have saved me financially, and it would have alleviated stress. Instead, it nearly cost me my business. The Scriptures remind us that there are seasons in our life when we need to downsize: There is "a time to get, and a time to lose; a time to keep, and a time to cast away." (Ecclesiastes 3:6)

Kingdom business owners don't only downsize for financial reasons; sometimes we downsize because we want to be in better alignment with God. As I've shared in other chapters, our success as Kingdom business owners is not based on financial gains alone. Yes, we're in business to prosper, and we don't want to be in financial bondage; however, it's important that we are rich in areas of our lives that are important to God.

If you downsize, you may temporarily lose money, but if you don't, you will lose something far more precious — your own children.

One of the biggest reasons we're slow to downsize is because we don't want to put down our pride, and we're afraid of what others will say. However, the more we struggle to grow when it's not our season, the more losses we will encounter financially, and the happier Satan will become. Satan always wants us to feel like we've failed. "Pride goes before destruction, and a haughty spirit before a fall." (Proverbs 16:18) Pride can hold you back from downsizing at the right time, which gives Satan an opportunity to rob you of your business. When you protect your business finances, you also protect your family relationships, your marriage, your health, and even your life.

ECCLESIASTES 3:1-8

To every thing there is a season, and a
time to every purpose under heaven:
A time to be born, and a time to die; a
time to plant, and a time to pluck that
which is planted;
A time to kill, and a time to heal; a time
to break down, and a time to build up;
A time to weep, and a time to laugh; a
time to mourn, and a time to dance;
A time to cast away stones, and a time
to gather stones together; a time to
embrace, and a time to refrain from
embracing;
A time to get, and a time to lose; a time
to keep, and a time to cast away;
A time to rend, and a time to sew; a time
to keep silence, and a time to speak;
A time to love, and a time to hate; a time
of war, and a time of peace.

Find Peace in Your Business

Operating from a constant state of overwhelm will cause your life to slowly break apart. Overload will cause heart attacks, strokes, and high blood pressure. Believe me, this is not God's Way. If your business is interfering with your relationship with God, it's time to make some changes. If your business is interfering with your health, you must know your life matters. If your business is taking you away from your family, downsizing or reallocating duties is the best option. So, as you can see, downsizing isn't about taking a financial loss; it's about winning in all areas of your life.

My dad, Apostle Winston Grier Sr., often told me, "Son, I don't want to be rich, but lying in a hospital bed from being overloaded, stressed, and exhausted. I don't want to be rich with no peace." He was teaching me the importance of being rich in all areas of my life.

Has your business threatened to destroy your marriage? Let me tell you, that's a BIG DEAL to God. Your business should never come between you and your spouse. The Scriptures state this clearly: "Therefore what God has joined together, let no man separate." (Mark 10:9)

Have you ever worked so much that before you realized it, your children are getting ready to graduate high school? If so, you are throwing the burden of your family responsibilities onto your spouse and kids while you succumb to stress, exhaustion, and eventually sickness. You may be making money, but you're not making money God's Way.

PSALM 37:23-24

The steps of a good man are ordered by the LORD, and He delights in his way. Though he fall, he shall not be utterly cast down; for the LORD upholds him with His hand.

JOHN 10:10

The thief does not come except to steal, and to kill, and to destroy. I have come that they may have life, and that they may have it more abundantly.

COLOSSIANS 3:15

And let the peace of God rule in your hearts, to which also you were called in one body; and be thankful.

Train Up Your Children

If you downsize, you may temporarily lose money, but if you don't, you will lose something far more precious — your own children. Your kids matter, and I don't want you to lose yours to street gangs, drugs, or anything else sent by Satan to destroy them.

Children are a gift from God, and you should be appreciative of this gift. Without your love and supervision, your children will suffer. But if you are there to support them, they will do better in school, and they will have greater opportunities for success once they graduate. The Scriptures tell us this: "Train up a child in the way he should go, and when he is old, he will not depart from it." (Proverbs 22:6) This training requires your time and attention. Do not hoard your business knowledge to yourself, for "Children are a heritage from the Lord." (Psalms 127:3) Instead, share what you know with your children, and you will ensure that the next generation will learn to do business God's Way.

> **Don't worry about the naysayers; the only One you need to worry about pleasing is God.**

Avoid Spiritual Poverty

Don't ever feel like a failure because you have chosen to downsize your business. Downsizing may be the difference between winning and losing for the Kingdom. The truth is this: If I have all the money in the world, yet I have no peace, I'm poor. If I have all the money in the world, yet I have no God, I'm poor. If I have all the money in the world, yet I lose my kids to gangs, I'm poor. If I have all the money in the world, yet I'm overwhelmed, stressed, and confused, I'm poor. This satanic poverty is bondage from the pits of hell. Downsizing can make you a winner in a losing situation and free you from bondage.

In conclusion, as you downsize, I want you to remember to live in peace in all areas of your life. Don't worry about the naysayers; the only One you need to worry about pleasing is God. When I decided to close down my tire shop and downsize, I didn't concern myself with what others had to say. The only One I owed an explanation to was God — my business partner. Others may judge you, but if you have good health, a sound mind, a happy family, and less debt, you're a winner, and Satan is defeated.

PHILIPPIANS 4:7

And the peace of God, which surpasses all understanding, will guard your hearts and minds through Christ Jesus.

MATTHEW 19:24

It is easier for a camel to go through the eye of a needle than for a rich man to enter the kingdom of God.

PROVERBS 22:6

Train up a child in the way he should go, and when he is old, he will not depart from it.

PROVERBS 16:7

When a man's ways please the LORD, He makes even his enemies to be at peace with him.

Pastor Grier's Humility Prayer for Your Business

Dear kind and heavenly Father, there will be times when I may have to put aside my pride and downsize my business. I know that I am doing this to save my family, my health, and ultimately my life. I ask that You would give me peace that surpasses all understanding to guard my heart and mind through Christ Jesus. (Philippians 4:6) God, I bind any spirit of worthlessness and depression that Satan will try to place in my heart and mind. Lord, I'm confident that soon enough, You will restore me as You promised in Joel 2:25: "And I will restore to you the years that the locust has eaten — the cankerworm, the caterpillar, and the palmerworm — My great army which I sent among you." All these blessings I ask for in Your son Jesus' name.

Amen.

8

**BE STEADFAST IN THE
WAYS OF THE LORD**

CHAPTER 8

Be Steadfast in the Ways of the Lord

Illegal Money, Illegal Business

A successful Kingdom business should strive to pursue financial freedom; however, our success is not judged solely by how much we have accrued in our time on earth. It is essential that we put just as much emphasis on our Kingdom account as we do our earthly account so that we may store up treasure in heaven. The Scriptures tell us this message clearly: "But lay up for yourselves treasures in heaven, where neither moth nor rust destroys and where thieves do not break in and steal." (Matthew 6:20)

I would like to share a little more about who I am. Yes, I'm a Pastor. However, I have not always been faithful to God. There was a time in my life when I was not obedient to God, and I didn't do things God's Way. I grew up a PK — a preacher's kid. My father, Apostle Winston Grier Sr., taught me all my young life to make Godly decisions.

Unfortunately, I was a hard-headed and re-bellious young man. I started looking at guys in the street with nice cars, fancy rims, and lots of money. As a kid, I thought to myself that I would love to have plenty of money the way those guys had it. In my 10th grade year, I left home; I turned to the streets and a life of crime. I began to sell drugs and do things that were embarrassing to my father and dishonorable to God. You may ask why the son of a bishop would turn to the streets. It was because Satan had gotten in my ear. Even though I was rich in the Spirit of the Lord, the devil made me feel impoverished. I was focused on making fast money. I wanted to get wealth and have finan-cial freedom, and Satan made me believe that the ends justified the means. Satan exploited the na-ivety of my young age and convinced me that this would position me in life a whole lot faster. I was ignorant, looking up to the wrong people, while being rebellious to my father. I didn't consider the consequences of my actions or the effect that I was having on my life and the lives of those around me. All I was thinking of was making money quickly.

PROVERBS 13:22

A good man leaves an inheritance to his children's children, but the wealth of the sinner is stored up for the righteous.

1 TIMOTHY 6:9-10

Those who desire to be rich fall into temptation and a snare, and into many foolish and harmful lusts which drown men in destruction and perdition. For the love of money is the root of all evil, for which some have strayed from the faith in their greediness, and pierced themselves through with many sorrows.

1 CORINTHIANS 15:58

Therefore, my beloved brothers, be steadfast, immovable, always abounding in the work of the Lord, knowing that in the Lord your labor is not in vain.

Shun the Love of Money

Many people will throw morals and biblical teaching away because of the love of money. Now, let me be clear — money itself is not evil. Making money allows us to best serve the Kingdom of God. No, it is the *love* of money that we must shun, "For the love of money is the root of all evil." (1 Timothy 6:10) Satan distracts us with our obsession over worldly matters, which turns us away from our service to the Lord.

At no point should we engage in illegal acts just for money. When we make money God's Way, we must ensure that our business follows the laws of the land. Illegal businesses are a detriment to the Kingdom. When I was selling drugs, I wasn't concerned about what the drugs were doing to my community. I desired money, and I was willing to pursue financial abundance by any means necessary.

Now, if you are running a legal business, you might think that my story doesn't apply to you. However, if you commit illegal acts within a legal business, you are still doing Satan's bidding. You must keep the devil from whispering in your ear, for he will take any opportunity to corrupt you with the love of money.

Some people may condemn me for speaking out against illegal business practices. They may judge me for making money God's Way. They may say that the Kingdom isn't important, and that the only thing that matters is self-enrichment. To these people, I say, "The Lord is our Judge, the Lord is our Lawgiver, the Lord is our King; He will save us." (Isaiah 33:22)

Wrong Is Wrong in the Eyes of the Lord

The Scriptures tell us in James 2:10: "For whoever shall keep the whole law, and yet stumble in one point, he is guilty of all." Wrong is wrong. Whether your illegal act is big or small, it's still wrong in the eyes of the Lord. Fortunately, our God is good and merciful. Although we are guilty of sin, He still allows us to ask for forgiveness and change our ways in the future.

In 2020, many people started fake businesses for the sole purpose of applying for and receiving money from Covid PPP and other government loans. So many individuals did this, in fact, that thousands of legal businesses were cheated out of these life-saving funds. There was no money left for the people who desperately needed it. Satan corrupted the hearts of these swindlers; they were so focused on their own financial gain that they lost any compassion that they had for the business owners who really needed help.

Now, I'm not judging anyone because we all have sinned, and there are times when we all come short of the glory. Rather, my aim in sharing this example is to highlight the corruption and destruction that result from the love of money. Greed causes people to make bad decisions that can cause far-reaching setbacks. Instead of boosting the US economy, many of these PPP loans vanished into the pockets of crooks. When thieves win, all honest businesses lose.

EZEKIEL 18:21-22

But if a wicked man turns
from all his sins which he
has committed, keeps all My
statutes, and does what is lawful
and right, he shall surely live;
he shall not die. None of the
transgressions which he has
committed shall be remembered
against him; because of the
righteousness which he has
done, he shall live.

PSALM 62:10

Do not trust in extortion or put vain
hope in stolen goods. If your riches
increase, do not set your heart on
them.

MATTHEW 5:19

Whoever therefore breaks one of
the least of these commandments,
and teaches men so, shall be called
least in the kingdom of heaven; but
whoever does and teaches them, he
shall be called great in the kingdom
of heaven.

Forgive Those Who Would Judge Your Past

Making Money God's Way is always the right path to financial freedom. Every day you wake up, the Lord gives you an opportunity to do business His Way. If you are a sinner, pray to God for His forgiveness; when you mend your ways, He will welcome you back into His fold.

There will always be people in your life who will bring up your past to harm your character, even when you've asked God for forgiveness and changed your life. I can attest to this. There are those who judge me for my sins, but I know that God is my only judge. As the Scriptures tell us, "Judge not, that you be not judged. For with what judgment you judge, you will be judged; and with the measure you use, it will be measured back to you. And why do you look at the speck in your brother's eye, but do not consider the plank in your own eye? Or how can you say to your brother, 'Let me remove the speck from your eye'; and look, a plank is in your own eye? Hypocrite! First remove the plank from your own eye, and then you will see clearly to remove the speck from your brother's eye." (Matthew 7:1–5)

God said to me one day, "Pastor, I do not judge you for your past drug dealing and failures. For have you not turned from your wicked ways? Have you not chosen to obey Me in all aspects of your life?" I told God, "Yes, Father. I have." Being able to answer "Yes" was relieving. In that moment, I knew that the Lord had forgiven me for my sins. Likewise, you may have memories of wrongdoing that you did to get money, but that is no longer your life. God has told me to tell you this: Hold your head high; do not beat yourself up, nor let people hold your past over your head. For you have been exonerated by God, and He is the only One that matters.

God's Way or No Way

In every field, there are businesspeople who decide to run their company through illegitimate means. There are some people who run their business without a proper license. There are other people who sell stolen goods. However, this kind of business operation doesn't line up with God because it breaks the law.

Being in alignment with God requires being obedient to the laws of the land. The Scriptures tell us, "Let every soul be subject to the governing authorities. For there is no authority except from God, and the authorities that exist are appointed by God. Therefore whoever resists the authority resists the ordinance of God, and those who resist will bring judgment on themselves." (Romans 13:1–2)

> **Wrong is wrong. Whether your illegal act is big or small, it's still wrong in the eyes of the Lord. Fortunately, our God is good and merciful.**

Obey the Laws of the Land

As a business owner, you will need to be licensed by your city and your state. Depending on your industry, you may also need to obtain certain governmental licenses, as well. For instance, my business requires that I have a scrap tire generator

ROMANS 13:7

Render therefore to all their due: taxes to whom taxes are due, revenue to whom revenue is due, respect to whom respect is due, honor to whom honor is due.

number. The EPA needs to have a count of all my tires so that they know I'm properly scrapping any tires that I don't sell. Every quarter, my business has to send in a report of how many tires we've sold and how many we've liquidated.

There are expenses associated with running your business in accordance with the laws of the land. For example, I need to pay the government a dollar for every tire I sell. If I sell 500 tires, I need to pay $500. There are other costs as well, and you need to know them all. They will eat into your profit if you don't keep track of them, and that can jeopardize your business.

Even if you unknowingly operate your business illegally, you are still out of alignment with God. You want to make sure that you're doing everything right according to the laws of the land as a Kingdom business owner. My advice to you is this: Hire the right professionals so you can run your business legitimately, and so that you don't spread yourself too thin trying to manage everything.

Obtain Business Insurance

Make sure that you have business insurance. If you don't, Satan will use it as an opportunity to rob you of your money with out-of-pocket expenses. For instance, if I towed someone's car without having business insurance, I would have to pay out of my own bank account if there were any issues. Since I have business insurance, both my customer and I are covered if the car incurs any damage during the towing process. Shop around for insurance. I went from paying $1100/month to $600/month for the same coverage when I looked for a better deal.

Hire Legal Representation

You also want to have good legal representation. You will need an attorney at your disposal to give you guidance. This doesn't have to be expensive. I pay less than $100/month to keep an attorney on retainer, and it is a tax write-off. It is an easy and inexpensive way to keep my business safe.

Pay Your Fair Share of Taxes

Another important part of doing business God's Way is paying your fair share of taxes. If you are dishonest with your money, you're also being dishonest with God.

In Matthew 22:21, Jesus said, "Render therefore unto Caesar the things which are Caesar's, and unto God the things that are God's."

In the same way, we must give Uncle Sam the money we own him. Pay your share and be honest when you do your taxes. You may be able to fool the government, but you can't fool God.

Do Right by God and He Will Increase for You

When you run your business honestly, you can be certain that the hard seasons you endure are just tests from God, like the tests that Job endured. You never want to be in the position where you have to ask, "Is God putting me through

JAMES 4:7

Submit yourselves therefore to God. Resist the devil, and he will flee from you.

PROVERBS 3:27

Do not withhold good from those to whom it is due, when it is in the power of your hand to do so.

ISAIAH 1:19

If you are willing and obedient, you shall eat the good of the land.

LUKE 11:28

Jesus said, "Blessed rather are those who hear the word of God and keep it!"

a trial to make me stronger? Or is he chastising me for engaging in bad business practices?"

When you do everything right by God, and then bad things happen, you know that God is getting ready to open up a promotion for you. Job was so confident in God because he knew that he lived his life in alignment with God's plan. Job said, "Though He slay me, yet will I trust in Him." (Job 13:15) He was sure that God would deliver him because he knew that he had done right by his business and his family.

Make Your Taxes Personal to You

An important part of doing business God's Way is doing the right thing even when nobody but God is watching you. Consider it a blessing that God has given you so much in your business that you can write a check and give more to the government. If I cheat the IRS and I pay $4,000, when the Lord has blessed me so well that I am able to pay $15,000, I may save money, but I won't be in alignment with God. However, if I render up to Caesar what is Caesar's, God will render to me what is mine. When I pay what I owe, I am confident that God will return it back to me tenfold. God is my business partner, and He will never let me down.

Make your taxes personal to you. The taxes you pay take care of people who make your business possible. They take care of the military, who are overseas protecting our country so we can run our businesses successfully. They take care of our police force, who keep our businesses safe from robbery when we are at home.

One night, when I was working late at my shop, a police officer stopped by to check and see if my building was secure. He explained that officers come by the area nightly to ensure that everything is safe. I was grateful that they were looking out for my business so that robbers wouldn't steal my tires or my equipment. My taxes pay for that protection.

When I pay my taxes, I think to myself, "I'm writing this check to the police officer who protects my shop when I'm asleep. I'm writing this check to the soldier who is protecting my country so I can run my business. These are the people that my money benefits."

The Bible says, "Thou shalt not steal." (Exodus 20:15) Every time we pay less than we owe, we are stealing from the people that allow our country to run.

On the flipside, don't overpay your taxes. A common way that businesses pay more than their share is when they don't itemize their business expenses. This is why you need to hire an accountant. Make sure that you have a professional who can help you manage your income and expenses. While you should render unto Caesar what is Caesar's, you don't need to give him a tip.

> You may have memories of wrongdoing that you did to get money, but that is no longer your life. God has told me to tell you this: Hold your head high; do not beat yourself up, nor let people hold your past over your head. For you have been exonerated by God, and He is the only One that matters.

Serve God, Not Money

Don't be a cheapskate. When you are miserly in your business, you are not serving God — you are serving money. As the Scriptures tell us, "No man can serve two masters." (Matthew 6:24) Do not let money separate you from the love of God. "Who shall separate us from the love of Christ? Shall tribulation, or distress, or persecution, or famine, or nakedness, or peril, or sword? ... Nor height, nor depth, nor any other creature, shall be able to separate us from the love of God, which is in Christ Jesus our Lord." (Romans 8:35, 39)

I have gotten into trouble before because I was thinking of money first before I thought of God. If you are a Kingdom person, this is unacceptable. We can't engage in worldly ways. Romans 12:2 tells us, "Be not conformed to this world, but be transformed by the renewing of your mind. Then you will be able to test and approve what is the good, pleasing, and perfect will of God."

You are a child of God. You should not blaspheme worldly people or look down on them, but neither should you join them. Instead, you must set a good example and dedicate yourself to doing business God's Way.

The Scriptures tell us, "For as a man thinks in his heart, so he is." (Proverbs 23:7) The way that you think will determine your actions. If you think like a worldly person, that is who you will be. When you set your mind to thinking the way that God wants you to, you are doing things God's Way.

Pastor Grier's Gratitude Prayer for Your Business

Dear kind and heavenly Father. Thank You for giving me a second chance. I pray that You will do the same for the person who is reading this book. God, we all have sinned, and we've all had times when we have come short of Your glory. And yet through it all, Your grace is sufficient. I'm grateful for Your unconditional love towards me and Your willingness to forgive my past failures. I pray, too, that You would put it in my heart to hold no judgment towards those who would judge me, for as the Scriptures say, "But if you do not forgive others their trespasses, neither will your Father forgive your trespasses." (Matthew 6:15) I am grateful that You have given me not "a spirit of fear, but rather one of power, and of love, and of a sound mind." (2 Timothy 1:7) All these blessings I ask for in Your son Jesus' name.

Amen.

9

SHARE YOUR WEALTH AND WEALTH SHALL BE SHARED WITH YOU

CHAPTER 9

Share Your Wealth and Wealth Shall Be Shared with You

Iron Sharpens Iron

Wealth is defined in the dictionary as "an abundance of valuable possessions or money." I believe that our knowledge, talents, and anointing are also forms of wealth. Our gifts are valuable possessions for us to share with others. Sharing wealth is not always about sharing money; wealth is anything of value that will help another person. There is nothing wrong with giving money, of course, and God will reward you for sharing your material wealth with those in need. However, there are times when God wants you to give knowledge or other valuable resources instead.

Teach a Man to Fish

God wants us to know about the many ways of sharing wealth, which He has laid out in the Scriptures. In Acts 3:2–7, the Bible tells us: "And a certain man lame from his mother's womb was carried, whom they laid daily at the gate of the temple which is called Beautiful, to ask alms from those who entered the temple; who, seeing Peter and John about to go into the temple, asked for alms. And fixing his eyes on him, with John, Peter said, 'Look at us.' So he gave them his attention, expecting to receive something from them. Then Peter said, 'Silver and gold I do not have, but what I do have I give you: In the name of Jesus Christ of Nazareth, rise up and walk.' And he took him by the right hand and lifted him up, and immediately his feet and ankle bones received strength."

This gentleman was lame from birth. If Peter and John had given him money, that would have been a nice temporary fix for his situation, but can you imagine how he felt being able to walk? He was now able to work and provide for himself for the rest of his life. This is similar to the saying, "Give a man a fish, and you feed him for a day. Teach a man to fish, and you feed him for a lifetime."

Our gifts are valuable possessions for us to share with others. Sharing wealth is not always about sharing money; wealth is anything of value that will help another person.

In Proverbs 16:16, the Bible says, "How much better to get wisdom than gold! And to get understanding is to be chosen rather than silver." This scripture reminds us that it's not only money we can share; there are other valuable resources we can offer that will be of great help to those around us. Peter and John shared their gift of

1 JOHN 3:17

But whoever has this world's goods, and sees his brother in need, and shuts up his heart from him, how does the love of God abide in him?

LUKE 6:37-38

Do not judge, and you will not be judged. Do not condemn, and you will not be condemned. Forgive, and you will be forgiven. Give, and it will be given to you. A good measure, pressed down, shaken together, and running over will be poured into your lap. For with the measure you use, it will be measured back to you.

PROVERBS 27:17

As iron sharpens iron, so a man sharpens the countenance of his friend.

anointing to heal, which allowed this once crippled man to arise and live a fulfilling life. The Scriptures tell us how happy this man was. "So he, leaping up, stood and walked and entered the temple with them — walking, leaping, and praising God. And all the people saw him walking and praising God." (Acts 3:8–9)

Enrich the Kingdom with Your Wisdom

I share this to remind you that you're a Kingdom business owner, and your wealth comes from God. You are called to share your wealth with others in the Kingdom so that they may glorify God and give Him the highest praise. It is especially important to share your gift of knowledge with other Kingdom businesspeople. In James 1:17, the Scriptures say, "Every good gift and every perfect gift is from above, and comes down from the Father of lights, with whom there is no variation or shadow of turning."

When you have obtained knowledge and wisdom (whether through experience or through education), this is a blessing from God. He has equipped you with the means to prosper, and He wishes for you to use this gift to help others succeed in life. God has not positioned you to be selfish; rather, He is calling on you to enlighten others how to prosper in their own life. In Proverbs 14:3, it is written, "In the mouth of a fool is a rod of pride, But the lips of the wise will preserve them." As a Kingdom businessperson, one of your most important jobs is to protect and care for your fellow brothers and sisters.

God tells us that it is important to share our money with those in need; however, if we give our brethren money but allow them to remain ignorant, it is like putting a band-aid on a broken leg. To have a wealth of knowledge is a blessing and gift from God, so use this blessing to bless others. When you enrich someone with your knowledge, you bless them with the means to make money God's Way. Their business will grow, and the Kingdom will increase as well.

Pull Your Brethren Out of Ignorance

As a Kingdom business coach, I take pride in teaching and mentoring others to help them improve their personal life, spiritual life, and business. If you do nothing else for God in your business, please reach out and help someone else by sharing what God has given you to succeed. For some businesspeople, it can be scary to share wisdom for fear that it will diminish their bottom line. However, Kingdom men and women should never operate in fear. The Scriptures tell us in 2 Timothy 1:7, "For God has not given us a spirit of fear, but of power and of love and of a sound mind."

Be confident that what God has for you is for you. Reach down, take someone by the hand, and pull them out of the ditch of ignorance so they may prosper God's Way. In Luke 4:18, the Scriptures say, "The Spirit of the Lord is upon Me, because He has anointed Me to preach the gospel to the poor; He has sent Me to heal the brokenhearted, to proclaim liberty to the captives and recovery of sight to the blind, to set at liberty those who are oppressed."

1 TIMOTHY 6:17-19

Command those who are rich in this present age not to be haughty, nor to trust in uncertain riches but in the living God, who gives us richly all things to enjoy. Let them do good, that they be rich in good works, ready to give, willing to share, storing up for themselves a good foundation for the time to come, that they may lay hold on eternal life.

I'm a Kingdom business owner, and I have the Holy Spirit inside of me, allowing the Lord to lead and guide me. Because of that, this is how I interpret this verse as a business owner: When I preach the Gospel to those who are poor in knowledge, I give them my wealth of wisdom so that through God, they can increase their finances. I motivate them with the lessons that God taught me during my most challenging times, and I encourage them to keep their faith in God, even in their darkest hour. God has shown me that by preaching deliverance to those who are held captive, we can lead them to liberty and financial freedom. We have a duty to give our brethren spiritual and business guidance that will free them from financial bondage and generational financial curses that are set out to destroy their business and the Kingdom.

By sharing your wealth in this way, you truly give sight to the blind. The Holy Spirit will speak through you to open other people's eyes to greater insight. As I've shared in this book, when I started out in business, I didn't have anyone that I could turn to. I believe that it is our responsibility to educate others on the dos and don'ts of business. Kingdom business owners should be glad to mentor or coach someone. The Scriptures tell us this in Galatians 6:7-9: "Whatever a man sows, that he will also reap. For he who sows to his flesh will of the flesh reap corruption, but he who sows to the Spirit will of the Spirit reap everlasting life. And let us not grow weary while doing good, for in due season we shall reap if we do not lose heart." This scripture reminds us that we are called to help others who are suffering. When you share your wealth, you get something of value in return, for "Whatever a man sows, that he will also reap." Give knowledge and you'll get it back, for you are never too old to learn.

DEUTERONOMY 8:18

And you shall remember the LORD your God, for it is He who gives you power to get wealth, that He may establish His covenant which He swore to your fathers, as it is this day.

PROVERBS 19:2

Desire without knowledge is not good — how much more will hasty feet miss the way!

COLOSSIANS 3:16

Let the word of Christ dwell in you richly in all wisdom, teaching and admonishing one another in psalms and hymns and spiritual songs, singing with grace in your hearts to the Lord.

LUKE 21:1-4

As Jesus looked up, He saw the rich putting their gifts into the temple treasury. He also saw a poor widow put in two very small copper coins. "Truly I tell you," He said, "this poor widow has put in more than all the others. All these people gave their gifts out of their wealth; but she out of her poverty put in all she had to live on."

PSALMS 133:1

Behold, how good and how pleasant it is for brethren to dwell together in unity!

LUKE 3:10-11

So the people asked him, saying, "What shall we do then?" John answered and said to them, "He who has two tunics, let him give to him who has none; and he who has food, let him do likewise."

Learn to Practice Humility

Don't ever feel like you need to know everything in order to run a business. Yes, you are the boss, but you will learn volumes from your employees and subordinates if you allow them to teach you. I remember I was working in my shop one evening alongside an employee whom I had trained. The job we were doing was challenging, and I was struggling to get it right. My employee looked up and saw that I was becoming frustrated. After a minute, he came over and asked me, "Hey, man, it looks like you could use some help. Do you want me to show you how I do it?"

Now, I could have said, "No, bro. I was the one who trained you, remember? I don't need your help." But that would have been foolish. It certainly wouldn't have made my job easier. So, I told him, "Of course. Please, show me your solution."

He taught me his way of doing the task, and I've been doing it his way ever since. God has taught me to practice humility, and that has been a lifesaver for me. God makes sure that when you give, it will come back to you, and your cup will begin to run over. "Give, and it will be given to you. A good measure, pressed down, shaken together, and running over will be poured into your lap. For with the measure you use, it will be measured back to you." (Luke 6:38)

> God tells us that it is important to share our money with those in need; however, if we give our brethren money but allow them to remain ignorant, it is like putting a band-aid on a broken leg.

Be Upfront with Your Customers

A few years after I opened my tire shop, I went into a local store to buy some items for my business. When I went to check out, the owner asked me, "Are you going to be paying with cash or credit?"

I told him that I would be using credit, and I asked him what the difference was. He said, "Well, just so you know, there's a 4% convenience fee added if you pay with debit or credit. If you would like to avoid the fee, you can pay in cash."

I didn't have enough cash on me, so I paid with credit. As I was swiping my card, I asked him, "Why do you charge an extra 4%? I haven't seen other companies doing that."

He told me, "I don't know if you realize this, but credit card companies charge businesses for every transaction."

I nodded. "I do know that. I run my own business."

He said, "Well, some businesses raise their rates on all their items to account for this. I've decided to add a 4% convenience fee to give customers the option of using credit in a way that doesn't impact my business. It's more beneficial to my customers than upping all my prices, and it gives customers the choice of avoiding the fee by paying cash. It's a win-win for everybody."

I looked into this, and I realized that it was a sensible strategy. The government doesn't permit businesses to charge a processing fee, but they do allow a convenience fee. I have incorporated this into my business, and it keeps me from losing money to the credit card companies while also offering my customers an option for saving money

JAMES 4:2-3

You lust and do not have. You murder and covet and cannot obtain. You fight and war. Yet you do not have because you do not ask. You ask and do not receive, because you ask amiss, that you may spend it on your pleasures.

HEBREWS 10:24-25

And let us consider one another in order to stir up love and good works, not forsaking the assembling of ourselves together, as is the manner of some, but exhorting one another, and so much the more as you see the Day approaching.

MARK 16:15

And He said to them, "Go into all the world and preach the gospel to every creature."

by paying in cash, or other less expensive payment methods. Before this, I had been paying over $500 a month in processing fees. Now, I use the savings to pay down my business debt or reinvest in my company. My customers appreciate that there's a way for them to cut costs, and I don't have to take money out of my pocket every time someone swipes their card.

Pastor Grier's Compassion Prayer for Your Business

Dear kind and heavenly Father, I pray that You would continue to give me the heart to help others grow in their business. Allow me to share my wisdom with those who are struggling for lack of knowledge. God, I realize that all I have comes from You. I came into this world with nothing, so everything I have You have supplied. My knowledge comes from You, Lord. My intellect about business comes from the experiences You have given me; my strength and perseverance come from Your will; and my financial wisdom comes from those You have allowed to pour into me. Dear Lord, I will repay You by helping those who are struggling financially. I will teach them how to walk in prosperity and be a blessing to Your Kingdom by sharing my wealth. All these blessings I ask for in Your son Jesus' name.

Amen.

10

COME TO GOD, ALL
WHO ARE WEARY, AND
HE WILL GRANT YOU
REST

CHAPTER 10

Come to God, All Who Are Weary, and He Will Grant You Rest

Enjoy God's Blessing of Rest

God knew we were going to have busy lives, and so in Genesis, He gave us an example to follow for how to rest. He gave us this example not because *He* needed it, but because He knew that *we* would. Every week, we must reserve some time to pause and celebrate God's goodness. God's primary reason for rest is for us to focus on the Kingdom. Hebrews 4:10 tells us, "For he who has entered His rest has himself also ceased from his works as God did from His." Therefore, it is for every believer to cease from his own work and fulfill his Kingdom duties.

Doctors, psychologists, and other experts in physical and mental health tell us how important rest is to our daily lives and the benefit it has for our mind and body. Rest gives us an opportunity to recharge mentally, physically, emotionally, and spiritually. But doctors are not the only ones telling us about the importance of rest. God wants us to be rich in every area of our lives, and rest allows us to achieve those riches.

God Doesn't Want You to Overwork Yourself

One day while running my 24/7 roadside business, I took a call to tow a vehicle. I was so overextended and exhausted that I could barely hold my eyes open while driving. God spoke to me and warned me, "Winston, stop overworking yourself. Get enough daily rest and don't forget your Sabbath duties. Satan wants you to fall asleep at the wheel and kill yourself or someone else. You must be more careful."

From that day on, I started looking at the Sabbath rest day differently. When you're on God's side, Satan will use the love of money to try and destroy you. One way he does this is by getting you to overwork yourself. However, you must remember that Kingdom business owners should only be money-driven within the context of Kingdom living. The Sabbath rest day is an ordained appointment with God. I call this my Weekly Partnership Meeting. Most business partners meet regularly, and the Sabbath day is your opportunity to meet with God and reflect on your accomplishments together. In this way, you

EXODUS 20:8-11

Remember the Sabbath day, to keep it holy. Six days you shall labor and do all your work, but the seventh day is the Sabbath of the Lord your God. In it you shall do no work: you, nor your son, nor your daughter, nor your male servant, nor your female servant, nor your cattle, nor your stranger who is within your gates. For in six days the Lord made the heavens and the earth, the sea, and all that is in them, and rested the seventh day. Therefore the Lord blessed the Sabbath day and hallowed it.

WINSTON GRIER

can find out whether you're still in alignment with God's vision for you, and you can learn how you can improve if needed.

God wants us to be certain that we are still following His plans for the Kingdom. If we miss our weekly meeting with God, we will get out of sync, which will give Satan an opportunity to lead us astray. When we take this time to rest on the Sabbath, it allows God to come to our aid. God reassures us, motivates us, and reminds us that we're in this together.

Do Not Eat the Bread of Anxious Toil

Years ago, one of my employees damaged my rollback tow truck. When I got the damage assessed, I found out it would cost me an arm and a leg to repair. I had to work seven days a week with no days off just to earn enough money to get my rollback fixed. I was exhausted, tired, and overloaded. I finally just sold my rollback at a discount to recoup some of my costs.

Later that week, I spoke to my dad about this frustrating experience. I told him that I'd had to sell my truck since I didn't have the money to get it repaired. My dad said to me, "Son why didn't you just put it on your insurance?"

Suddenly, I realized my mistake. I had a one-million-dollar auto liability, as well as general liability plus cargo, but this never came to my mind because I was working round the clock and was mentally overloaded. I had just sold my truck for pennies on the dollar because I couldn't afford the full repair costs, without realizing that my insurance would cover repairs from damages done by my employees with only a small deductible. I honestly believe that if I had taken a day of rest, the Lord would have given me this revelation about my insurance. I want everyone to understand how important rest is to your success. You cannot do your best if you are working yourself into the ground. God took a day off, and we should too.

I grew up in a home where my parents believed in the importance of Sabbath rest. My father, Apostle Winston Grier Sr., and my mother would prepare the day before the Sabbath. They looked forward to this time to relax, be in God's presence, worship, pray together, and visit our elderly family and friends in the nursing home. Satan will try his best to rob you of God's time, so you need to plan for your days of rest like you are preparing for an appointment with God. For example, my dad and mom would stay away from any worldly distractions on God's Day. My dad didn't even check his mailbox. He didn't want to open a bill and have Satan try to rob him of his appreciation for God's goodness. I'm not suggesting you do exactly as my parents did, but I am recommending that you set aside a time for the Lord each week, however God leads you.

> When you're on God's side, Satan will use the love of money to try and destroy you. One way he does this is by getting you to overwork yourself. However, you must remember that Kingdom business owners should only be money-driven within the context of Kingdom living.

GENESIS 2:2-3

And on the seventh day God ended His work which He had done, and He rested on the seventh day from all His work which He had done. Then God blessed the seventh day and sanctified it, because in it He rested from all His work which God had created and made.

HEBREWS 4:11

Let us, therefore, make every effort to enter that rest, so that no one will perish by following their example of disobedience.

PSALM 127:2

It is in vain that you rise up early and go late to rest, eating the bread of anxious toil; for He gives to His beloved sleep.

Make Time to Rest and Reflect

Rest in God, rest your body, rejuvenate your mind, and enjoy the things God has gifted you with.

Here is what I choose to do on my Sabbath rest day:

- Study God's Word.
- Pray and meditate.
- Enjoy my family and friends.
- Visit and pray for the sick.
- Visit prisoners to give them God's Word.

Spend time with your family. Your kids will grow older, so enjoy them while they're young. You will lose loved ones, so cherish those moments. Your health will come and go in seasons, so enjoy it when you have it. You will need God's guidance for direction, so rest in His Word, meditate, and listen to His direction concerning your life and your business.

Allow yourself to have one day out of the week where you don't focus on the intricacies of making money. You have an opportunity to pause and worship. Reflect on the goodness of God and everything that He has done for you.

Follow God's Example

In the beginning, God labored for six days, and on the seventh day, He ceased from all His works. He is our example. He rested on the seventh day to show us the importance of ceasing from work.

He intends for us to have a day where we meditate on Him. This is time to read our Bibles, reflect on the Lord's goodness, and give thanks for all the things that He has done for us.

On the Sabbath, it is essential to shift your focus from money to God. There was a time in my life where I worked for seven days a week, chasing money. I worked so much that I quickly reached diminishing returns. I didn't accomplish as much as I wanted to financially. My body was worn down, and my mind was exhausted. When you are overloaded, it is hard to think about positive ways to prosper. You have done too much, and you've overrun yourself.

If you want to make money God's Way, you must remember that "the blessing of the Lord makes you rich, and He adds no sorrow with it." (Proverbs 10:22) Working seven days a week with no days off is filled with sorrows, which means that it is not Godly. Be obedient to God and observe His Sabbath. I can promise you that you are not missing out on any sales. Anything God intends for you, He will make sure that you receive. Remember, God is your business partner. When you abide by His Word, He will ensure that your business will flourish.

> **Spend time with your family. Your kids will grow older, so enjoy them while they're young. You will lose loved ones, so cherish those moments. Your health will come and go in seasons, so enjoy it when you have it. You will need God's guidance for direction, so rest in His Word, meditate, and listen to His direction concerning your life and your business.**

Take Inspiration from Successful Businesses

A business that inspires me is Chick-fil-A. They implement a day off where they close all their franchises and allow their employees to rest. They set aside that day to give their team the opportunity to worship God and reflect on His goodness. Now, this doesn't hurt their business at all. In fact, it has improved their bottom line. When I look at the restaurants in my community, for instance, I always see my neighborhood Chick-fil-A overflowing with customers. Their employees are in good spirits and very polite. People are willing to wait in line for their Chick-fil-A meals, and the day after their rest day, business is always booming.

It is clear to me that God is doing something for this franchise. Chick-fil-A is one of the top ten fast food restaurants according to gross. So, take their example. Give yourself some time to rest and be with God. The Lord will compensate you for honoring Him. I can promise you, when you obey God and enjoy the respite He intends for you, He will send customers and sales to you in abundance on all the other days you're open.

HEBREWS 4:9-10

There remains therefore a rest for the people of God. For he who has entered His rest has himself also ceased from his works as God did from His.

ISAIAH 30:15

For thus says the Lord GOD, the Holy One of Israel: "In returning and rest you shall be saved; In quietness and confidence shall be your strength."

Come to Me, all you who labor and are heavy laden, and I will give you rest. Take My yoke upon you and learn from Me, for I am gentle and lowly in heart, and you will find rest for your souls. For My yoke is easy and My burden is light.

Pastor Grier's Respite Prayer for Your Business

Dear Kind and Heavenly Father, every day I desire to be more like You. In Genesis 2:1-3, You rested from all Your works. My desire is to have a day where I can reflect on Your goodness, rest in Your presence, and be thankful for all the blessings that You have bestowed on my business and my family. Lord, I'm thanking You for Your goodness, everything that You have done for me, the favor that You have granted me, and the grace and mercy that You have given me. I thank You and honor You for being the guiding force in my life. I rest to bless Your name, honor You as the God of Heaven and earth, and remember where my blessings and favor come from. Lord, no matter how much money I make in my business, I will pause to enjoy the day that You have set aside for me and my family. All these blessings I ask for in Your son Jesus' name.

Amen.

11

JIREH, YOU ARE ENOUGH

CHAPTER 11

Jireh, You Are Enough

From Defeated to Winning

Many years ago, I was in bankruptcy. I was struggling to keep up with my payments, but the judge in charge of my case gave me only thirty days to catch up, or they would have to repossess everything that I had — my business tire equipment, my trucks, and my vehicles. I prayed to God for him to intercede for me financially so I wouldn't lose my business. As a child, my parents taught me to go to God for what you need, as it says in the Scriptures: "The name of the LORD is a strong tower; the righteous run to it and are safe." If nothing else, I needed to be safe.

Finally, my court date arrived. The bankruptcy judge had me in strict compliance. I didn't have the money, and I was scared to go to court emptyhanded. I knew my livelihood was at stake. I was sitting on my front porch, feeling like a failure. I prayed to God, asking Him, "Lord, why is this happening to me?" I was so disappointed because I felt that if God had allowed me to earn even half the money to make my payments, I could have talked the judge into giving me some additional time to pay the remaining half. Unfortunately, that didn't happen. So, there I was, sitting on my porch, and I decided not to go to court. After all, I thought to myself, what was the use? I didn't have any money, and I knew this judge was very strict. If I didn't have my full payment, they would repossess everything. I tried to figure out how I was going to tell my wife that they would even take my Chrysler 300 that she drove.

I began to talk to God and said, "Lord, I trust You, and I still have faith in You, but I don't understand why I am going through this."

God said to me, "Get up and finish your faith."

I perceived that God was saying go on to court, broke, with no money, which seemed crazy to me. However, I got in my car, and I headed to Augusta, Georgia.

My attorney saw me when I walked in and asked me, "Winston, do you have your money?"

"No, sir," I said.

"Well, how much do you have?" he asked.

"I don't have anything," I said, shaking my head. This made me even more disappointed because I knew that my lawyer couldn't fight for me when I gave him nothing to work with. I explained to my attorney that my business had been very, very slow. He told me that this judge would not give an extension. I said, "I completely understand."

A few minutes later, the judge called me up. She asked my attorney, "Does your client have his full payment?"

And the Lord restored Job's losses when he prayed for his friends. Indeed the Lord gave Job twice as much as he had before. Then all his brothers, all his sisters, and all those who had been his acquaintances before, came to him and ate food with him in his house; and they consoled him and comforted him for all the adversity that the Lord had brought upon him. Each one gave him a piece of silver and each a ring of gold. And the Lord blessed the latter days of Job more than his beginning.

"No, your honor," replied my attorney.

The judge held her head down, and when she held it back up, she said, "Winston, I don't normally do this, but I'm going to give you 90 days to get this paid off."

I walked out of the courtroom with tears in my eyes, grateful that I had trusted in God's command and didn't stay home, even though it had seemed crazy to go to court without any money. God had softened the judge's heart, and she was lenient, even though she didn't have to be. She gave me a 90-day extension, which allowed me to pay back what I owed. Satan had tried to get me to give up on God, but if I had listened to the devil, I would have lost everything.

Children obey their parents, and so we must obey God our Father. If I had not obeyed God, the judge wouldn't have offered me such leniency in the courtroom. Even when you are suffering with bad credit or no money, know that it's not the end of the world. Obey God and ask Him for forgiveness, and He will provide you His grace.

When I walked out of the courtroom, my attorney came over to me and asked, "Do you know her, Winston?"

"No, sir," I replied.

My attorney shook his head. "Wow. I've been coming to this courtroom in front of her for over fifteen years, and she's never done this before. Are you sure you don't know her?" He was so amazed and in disbelief that he went back to make sure with the clerk that the judge had granted me an extension. I had prayed to God to send money, but instead He sent me grace and favor. He told me to go to court that day so that He could show me how He works in my life.

I had an opportunity to file Chapter 7, Chapter 11 or Chapter 13 Bankruptcy. I chose Chapter 11 because that allow me to pay my creditors. I also made a promise to my loan officer that I would pay everything that I owed the bank. I kept my word. In ten days, I paid it off and went to Louisville to the bank headquarters to receive all my titles. Leaving the bank was an emotional moment for me because I knew it was all due to God. I left the bank with my titles for my truck, my car, my mobile utility trailer, and all my tire equipment. I left there with everything that belongs to me. Satan tried to take it all, but God protected, God promised, and God provided. I'm not bragging on myself because it was nothing that I did. It was not because I was the businessman of the year, but because every time I wanted to give up, God would just keep covering me. This lesson taught me to never give up on God nor your business, even when things look impossible.

I learned a valuable lesson from these experiences. I didn't have the money, but I didn't need money — I needed God. My attorney thought I came to court emptyhanded, but I had everything because I had faith in a loving God. God gave me these hardships to remind me that when I have nowhere to turn, He is all I need. I'm grateful that when I don't have the money or the credit, Jireh, you are enough.

The Lord your God will make you abound in all the work of your hand, in the fruit of your body, in the increase of your livestock, and in the produce of your land for good. For the Lord will again rejoice over you for good as He rejoiced over your fathers, if you obey the voice of the Lord your God, to keep His commandments and His statutes which are written in this Book of the Law, and if you turn to the Lord your God with all your heart and with all your soul.

God Will Test You in Your Business

When you're a kingdom business owner, God will sometimes use your suffering for his glory. You can do everything right in your business, and still God will give Satan permission to test you.

I want to tell you about such a person — his name was Job. He was a businessman that scripture tells us did everything right. In Job 1:1–3, the Bible tells us that, "There was a man in the land of Uz, whose name was Job; and that man was blameless and upright, and one who feared God and shunned evil. And seven sons and three daughters were born to him. Also, his possessions were seven thousand sheep, three thousand camels, five hundred yoke of oxen, five hundred donkeys, and a very large household, so that this man was the greatest of all the people of the East."

When you read the first chapter of Job, the Bible says that Job lost everything that he had. He had the biggest farm business on the East side of the world. His farm was large, even by modern standards. In today's words, we would say that Job owned a major corporation.

Now, Job lost everything, but this wasn't because he had done something wrong. He was a good man and God-fearing. Rather, Job was someone who God used as a test.

The Bible tells us, "There was a day when the sons of God came to present themselves before the Lord, and Satan also came among them." (Job 1:6)

When God saw Satan in their midst, he asked the devil what his purpose was here on earth. Satan replied that he was roaming the earth to see who he could corrupt and destroy.

God asked the devil, "Have you considered My servant Job, that there is none like him on the earth?" (Job 1:8)

God trusted Job so much, He was so confident in Job's faith, that He gave Satan the invitation to try and destroy him.

Satan asked God, "Does Job fear You for nothing? Have You not made a hedge around him, around his household, and around all that he has on every side? You have blessed the work of his hands, and his possessions have increased in the land. But now, stretch out Your hand and touch all that he has, and he will surely curse You to Your face!" (Job 1:9–11)

> When you experience hardship and pain, know that God has not turned His back on you. He puts you through these trials and challenges because He trusts you to rise above and grow stronger in your faith.

Satan saw that God had blessed Job with plenty of money and land; in fact, He had given Job everything that he desired. So, Satan wagered that Job was only loyal to God because his life was good; he didn't believe that Job was a true servant of God.

As people of God, we will sometimes be put in a similar position. A millionaire might find it easy to say, "I love the Lord my God with all my heart, with all my soul, and with all my mind." (Matthew 22:37) But would you still maintain that same love for God if you lost everything? Would you still serve God if all your wealth disappeared?

God told Satan, "Everything he has is in your hands," (Job 1:12) and He invited Satan to test Job.

In the same way, there will come a time when God will give Satan the invitation to test us as business owners. But as Kingdom people, our worship and our love for God must not change.

JOB 1:8

Then the Lord said to Satan,
"Have you considered My servant
Job, that there is none like him on
the earth, a blameless and upright
man, one who fears God and
shuns evil?"

DEUTERONOMY 8:18

And you shall remember the Lord your
God, for it is He who gives you power
to get wealth, that He may establish
His covenant, which He swore to your
fathers, as it is this day.

JOB 2:6

He is in your hands, but you must
spare his life.

As a Pastor and a Kingdom businessman, I tell you this: My relationship with God doesn't change because my pockets are empty. My love for God doesn't change because I lost a few sales or contracts. We will all have times in our life when Satan will come to us, and God will give him permission to test us.

The Bible says in 1 Peter 4:1, "As Christ has suffered for us in the flesh, arm yourselves likewise with the same mind: for he that has suffered in the flesh has ceased from sin."

This means that you, too, as a Kingdom person will have times of suffering in your life. However, this is not because God is punishing you; rather, it is because He is testing you. When you experience hardship and pain, know that God has not turned His back on you. He puts you through these trials and challenges because He trusts you to rise above and grow stronger in your faith.

God Will Not Allow Satan to Destroy Your Business

Satan tested Job, and even after he took everything from him, Job still didn't curse God. Satan took Job's property, his servants, his children, and his health, and yet Job stayed faithful to God.

Satan went back to God and said, "Stretch out Your hand now, and touch his bone and his flesh, and he will surely curse You to Your face!" (Job 2:5)

Yet here, God stopped Satan in his tracks. He said, "He is in your hands, but you must spare his life." (Job 2:6)

God allowed Satan to test Job, but He protected Job from death. This part is important. It means that God is in total control of what you are going through. God told Satan that he could do what he wished to Job, but Job's life was not Satan's to take. Now, as a Kingdom business owner, you know that your life is your business. Satan may take all your contracts and your customers, but he can't take your business. Your business may go through hard seasons, but God won't let you fail.

You may have a period when your credit may not be good enough, and your money may run low, and yet when you stay connected with God and you trust Him with all your heart, He will repay you in abundance. He will put you through tests, but He won't allow you to be destroyed.

Never Give Up on God

Never give up on God, for He has not abandoned you. You can do everything right, and you will still get tested. Remember, the Bible tells us that Job "was blameless and upright, and one who feared God and shunned evil." In all things, he refrained from doing wrong. He feared God, meaning that he did whatever God commanded. This was a man who was perfect, and yet he lost everything. He was obedient, and yet he was catching hell on earth.

Now, Job could have protested. He could have easily cursed God and said, "Lord, I've done everything you've asked me to do. I am upright in my business, and I am a good husband and father. I curse you for being so unfair to me!"

But Job shows us that we never have the right to give up on God. He had confidence because he knew that he had done right by God. He never faltered in his faith. Even if we are at the lowest point in our life, we mustn't turn our backs on Him.

Whenever you're going through hard times, so long as you've been doing right by God, He will see you through. Once you pass God's testing of you, He will reward you tenfold. Your cup will begin to run over.

Stay Constant and Patient in Your Worship

Now, I want to warn you that the people around you may not understand what you are going through, even members of your own family. Job's wife didn't understand that God was testing Job, and she grew frustrated and impatient. One day, she said to Job, "Do you still hold fast to your integrity? Curse God and die!" (Job 2:9)

But Job did not curse God. Instead, he said to his wife, "You speak as a foolish woman speaks. Shall we accept good from God, and yet not accept adversity?" (Job 2:10)

When Job's wife told him to "curse God and die," Job knew that Satan was speaking through her. Satan will do what he can to cut you off from God. The devil was able to get his hooks into Job's wife because she got impatient. Satan looks for our impatience — when he sees it, he will use it as an entry point into our heart and mind.

Job's wife behaved like most worldly people would. She was talking out of disappointment. She was tired of seeing her husband suffer when he had been so obedient. She couldn't fathom why he was catching so much hell when he had been such a good servant to God.

Similarly, you may have had someone in your life tell you, "That's enough. I'm tired of hearing about all this God stuff." Yet when you have a connection with God and you trust Him, you know that whatever dark passage the Lord is leading you through, He will carry you out the other side. That's what shook Satan's foundation. He saw that Job stood firm and wouldn't let go of his faith.

Job knew that everything he possessed belonged to God. He said, "Naked I came into this world, and naked I shall return. The Lord gave, and the Lord has taken away. Blessed be the name of the Lord." (Job 1:21)

When you come here, you come here with nothing. Everything that you own, everything that you have now, you got it from God. That's why the Bible says in Deuteronomy 8:18, "And you shall remember the Lord your God, for it is He who gives you power to get wealth, that He may establish His covenant, which He swore to your fathers, as it is this day."

I want you to know that as a Kingdom person, sometimes you will go through trials and tests that will cause you to suffer. But still, you must serve God. In Isaiah 6:8, the Bible says, "I heard the voice of the Lord, saying: 'Whom shall I send? And who will go for Us?' Then I said, 'Here am I! Send me'." In the same way, when you pray to God and say, "Here I am, Lord. Use me for Your glory," the Lord is going to use you.

Never give up on God, for He has not abandoned you. You can do everything right, and you will still get tested.

Job never cursed God, even in the midst of everything that he was going through. Instead, the Bible tells us, "Then Job arose, tore his robe, and shaved his head; and he fell to the ground and worshiped." (Job 1:20)

Some people, when their business is doing poorly, they stop going to church, and they stop

JOB 1:21

Naked I came into this world, and naked I shall return. The Lord gave, and the Lord has taken away. Blessed be the name of the Lord.

praising God. As long as their business is thriving, they proclaim, "I'm blessed, I'm highly favored, I'm ready to serve the Lord." But you've got to serve God even when you're having hard days, hard weeks, and hard seasons. As a Kingdom person, your worship for God shouldn't change. That's what sets you apart from worldly people.

Ask God to Co-sign for You

Throughout his trials, Job still tried to maintain his business, even as he grew weaker. He said, "My spirit is broken, my days are extinguished, the grave is ready for me." (Job 17:1) Then he prayed to God, "Now put down a pledge for me with Yourself. For who is he who will shake hands with me?" (Job 17:3)

What Job meant was, "Lord, I ask You to co-sign for me." Back in the days of the Bible, when someone shook hands with you, it meant they promised to be honest in their business dealings with you. Job knew that no one would do business with him (shake hands) or give him a loan (a pledge) without God's support. After all, he had lost everything, and any reasonable lender would see him as insolvent. In today's words, we would say that Job was broke and had terrible credit.

I share this scripture to remind you that even when your finances are in disarray, you can go to God just like Job did. As a Kingdom business owner, you must humble yourself before God as Job did and tell Him, "Lord, I ask you to co-sign for me. Open up the door for me."

The Bible says, "The earth is the Lord's, and the fulness thereof; the world, and they that dwell therein." (Psalm 24:1) Let me tell you, when you have a co-signer like God, the Creator of Heaven and Earth, the One who owns everything, you have a mighty partner in your business. When you have a co-signer like God, you have nothing to worry about.

Job was so patient with God. In Job 13:15, he said, "Though He slay me, yet will I trust Him. Even so, I will defend my own ways before Him."

In the same way, you may be going through hard times, and yet you must still trust in the ways of the Lord. When you are building your business and you have neither money nor credit, all you need is God on your side. You can still succeed when you ask God to put his name up for you. Just have faith and focus on doing things God's Way. The Lord will hold your business up even when Satan wants it to crumble to the ground.

Pray Even for Those Who Disparage You

When you read Job, you will see that his friends and acquaintances pulled away from him. Even his family left. All those who loved him when he had everything abandoned him when he had nothing. Even so, Job remained true to those he loved.

In Job 42:10, the Bible says, "And the Lord restored Job's losses when he prayed for his friends. Indeed, the Lord gave Job twice as much as he had before."

God restored what Job had lost by twofold, and look at when the Bible tells us He did this: it was when Job prayed for his friends. Now, the Bible tells us that Job's friends distanced themselves from him. They believed that he had lost God's favor.

After all, he had no more money, he had creditors after him, and his family was torn asunder. And yet Job prayed for his friends, even though these were the people who had been speaking ill of him.

My message for Kingdom business owners is this: you may have a time when it seems like you are about to go out of business. However, God is just setting you up for getting double of what you had. He is setting you up for more. You may lose ten contracts, but God will pay you back with twenty.

When you pray even for those who have disparaged you, God will reward you in abundance.

God Is Partnering with You Against Satan

When I ponder this chapter, I notice the scripture reminds us that Job feared God, he refrained from wrongdoing, he lived righteously, and yet he couldn't avoid catching hell on earth. I quickly saw myself in Job's story because I have been there. I lost money, I lost my good credit, and I lost contracts. I was living for God.

I asked God during my meditation, "Lord, what does this mean to live right and still have trying times?" God said to me, "I was so proud of Job that I gave Satan an invitation to challenge him because Satan thought Job's love for Me was based on money and possessions. I allowed Job to lose everything because I had confidence that regardless of what I took Job through, he wouldn't embarrass Me."

When we become successful, Satan will test us as part of his scheme to destroy the Kingdom.

Satan saw that Job had achieved great heights, which meant that he had a long way to fall. The devil believed that Job would curse God as soon as he lost his wealth, and if other men saw the most pious Job curse God, they would be more likely to abandon God, as well. In the same way, Satan will try to get Kingdom people to curse God, so that others will turn away from His righteous path. We must not fall for Satan's schemes. We have to live up to the example set by Job so that God will have full confidence in our faith.

Too often, we jump to the conclusion that God has abandoned us when we suffer misfortune, but this couldn't be further from the truth. In reality, God is showing us how much he trusts us. He is partnering with us against Satan.

> **When you are building your business and you have neither money nor credit, all you need is God on your side. You can still succeed when you ask God to put his name up for you.**

He is putting us forward as someone for the devil to test so that we can join forces with the Lord to defeat the enemy.

God often puts us Kingdom people through tests. It's like when you were in school. You couldn't advance to the next grade until you had passed all your exams. This is God's way of increasing your abundance, not only in your finances, but also in your anointing, so that you can get ready for greater works.

God wants us to grow in our ability to serve the Kingdom. When we make it through these trials and receive our rewards from God, we put Satan in his place, and we show the rest of the Kingdom the goodness of the Lord.

In Job 19:25, Job said, "For I know that my redeemer lives, and that He shall stand at the

JOB 17:3

Now put down a pledge for me
with Yourself. For who is he who
will shake hands with me?

JOB 42:10

And the Lord restored Job's losses
when he prayed for his friends.
Indeed, the Lord gave Job twice as
much as he had before.

JOB 19:25

For I know that my redeemer lives,
and that He shall stand at the latter
day upon the earth.

latter day upon the earth." He knew that God would stand up for him. Even when he was going through all his trials, he knew that God was beside him, protecting him.

The Book of Job shows us as Kingdom business people just what God can do for us when we keep the faith in Him and trust Him: You may make mistakes. Your credit score may fall. Your money may vanish into thin air. But when you've got God on your side, when you trust in God and remain faithful and obedient to Him, He won't let you fail.

Understanding the Lesson of Job

Do not mistake the lesson of Job as one of God being against wealth. God wants you to prosper. He will not punish you for earning money. You can have millions of dollars in your business, and so long as you have a good relationship with God, He will reward you.

Instead, the lesson is this: If your business is prosperous, and you and your family are thriving, Satan will most certainly come knocking on your door. The devil will try to destroy your relationship with God by destroying your business. He's aiming to kill two birds with one stone. He wants you to give up all hope so that you will curse God and die. His ultimate goal is to separate you from God.

Satan destroyed Job's business as a means to an end. That's why he kept inflicting Job with worse and worse punishments. If Job had immediately cursed God after Satan destroyed his business, Satan would have simply declared victory and gone gloating to God. Job went through as many trials as he did because of the strength of his faith. He said, "Though He slay me, yet will I trust Him." (Job 15:13) In the same way, allow each test that you endure to bolster your faith and make your loyalty to God that much stronger than before.

Doing Business God's Way

When we do business God's Way, it's not all about making money. Yes, we want to be successful, we want to be financially secure, but we can't lose our relationship with God because we don't have wealth. We can't let feelings of scarcity and lack diminish our love and worship towards God. Our relationship with God still must stand firm, regardless of how many zeros come after the number in our bank account.

Doing things God's way is completely different than doing things in a worldly way. Yes, God wants you to increase financially, but he also wants you to grow spiritually. We have to remember that in order to advance to those spiritual levels that God has set for us, we've got to be tested. We must pass our tests to get promoted. Going through those trying times is like interviewing for a better position in a company. When you pass your interview, you reach the next level.

Remember, God chose Job not because he thought that Job was doing something wrong; rather, he chose Job specifically because he was doing everything right. He knew that Job would be able to pass all His tests. He chose Job because He was confident that Job would be able to thwart Satan's schemes.

You see, it's one thing to have your boss confident in you, or to have your spouse confident

JOB 15:13

Though He slay me, yet will I trust Him.

JOHN 6:27

Do not labor for the food which perishes, but for the food which endures to everlasting life, which the Son of Man will give you, because God the Father has set His seal on Him.

in you, but it's something else entirely to have God confident in you. God showed just how much He trusted Job by allowing Satan to test him, knowing that Satan would fail.

In Job, we find a pure example of a Kingdom businessman's trust in God. Our worship mustn't stop when we go broke or get a bad credit score; instead, we must trust our business partner to bring us out. You see, not only did God have faith in Job, but Job had faith in God. When we partner with someone, we must have confidence in them. It doesn't do us any good to partner with someone that we don't trust. Job had confidence in his partner. He knew that God wasn't going to let his business fail. He knew that his partner was going to lift him back up. Your partnership with God must be one of mutual trust between both you and the Lord.

In my business, I trust God, and He trusts me. When people driving through my city break down by the side of the road, God sends them to me because He has confidence that I will take care of them.

As Kingdom business owners, we must strive to do right by God every day. When God sends customers our way, we must show Him that we are trustworthy by taking care of those customers as if they were our own family.

Sometimes we miss opportunities because we don't have the integrity that God wants us to have. If we lack that integrity, God won't allow people to come our way. But when God has confidence that we will be fair and treat people right, He will let our doors stay open. That's what it takes to grow our business and bring it to the next level. By following the lessons of Job, we see how to run an upstanding Kingdom business that will increase and allow us to have more than enough.

Pastor Grier's Devotion Prayer for Your Business

Dear kind, and heavenly Father. I want to thank You for being faithful to me even when I'm not faithful. Lord, I ask for Your forgiveness in my weakest hour when I want to give up on my business. Lord, thank You for Your protection, provision, and power. Dear Lord, help me to remain steadfast and trust You, regardless of what I'm up against. God, You are my strength, my redeemer, my everything, and there is none like You. God, every time I experience lack, You constantly remind me that You are enough, and for that I thank You. All these blessings I ask for in Your son Jesus' name.

Amen.

12

PASTOR GRIER'S
TESTIMONY

CHAPTER 12

Pastor Grier's Testimony

Faith Lost and Faith Regained

When I was eleven years old, my mother was diagnosed with cancer. She got sick very quickly, and I felt helpless watching her get weaker and weaker. I grew up in a household of faith. My Dad is Apostle Winston Grier Sr., and he was the pastor of my church growing up. After my mother's diagnosis, my Dad would lead us in prayers to ask God to spare my Mom's life. We would pray throughout the day, and at night as well.

My Mom's cancer was very aggressive, and she passed not long after she was diagnosed. God ended her pain, and He brought her home to Him.

However, as a twelve-year-old kid, I didn't have context for understanding this. All I knew was that I had prayed to the Lord every day for my mother to live, but instead of sparing her life, God had taken her away from me. I was very disappointed and angry at God.

I'm sharing my story with you because I want to show you how the Lord works. I want you to know that sometimes you may not get the answer that you want from God. However, God is always right. He may not give you the answer you desire, but He will always give you the answer you need.

You see, I've been studying the Bible for nearly my entire life, ever since I was able to read. By the time I was twelve years old, I had been reading the Bible for seven years. My Dad raised us in a family of faith. I owe my understanding of God's Word to him. At five years old, I knew all sixty-six Books of the Bible. I knew the Scriptures and the Stories. My parents taught us to sing the Books of the Bible, and when my Dad asked us questions, he expected us to know the answers.

> I was taught that if you prayed honestly, God would hear you and He would answer your prayer.

As a child, I had read so many stories about God's ability to heal. I read about the lame man who was sick and unable to walk, I read about the blind man who couldn't see, I read about the woman who was deathly ill, and I saw God heal all these people. The lame man stood up and walked, the blind man gained the ability to see, the sick woman was healed from the issue of blood. So, as a twelve-year-old kid, I was in expectation of God's ability to do the same thing for my family. I believed that God would heal my Mom from her cancer.

My Dad was a preacher at two churches at the time, and my siblings and I would always go with my Dad when he preached the Word. All of my brothers and sisters played instruments at church, but since I was the oldest boy, my Dad would let me stay with my Mom. I would sit with my Mom and pray with her. I was able to see how ill she was. She would get these sharp pains, and sometimes she would start crying. Here I was, this twelve-year-old boy, and I didn't know what to do. It was one of the greatest struggles of my life.

I had a school teacher in sixth grade. Her name was Miss Wilcher. We used to call her Miss Barbara. She really helped me to keep going when my Mom was sick. She was very encouraging. Every Friday before we left for the weekend, she would always say, "Winston, are you okay?" And I would always reply, "Yes, ma'am." I couldn't really tell her what was happening in my family or what was going on with my relationship with God because I didn't fully understand any of it myself. Still, she would pull me out into the hallway to check in with me. She would ask how I was doing, or how my day was going. She was a very caring teacher. She asked me because she was genuinely concerned about me. Looking back, I really appreciate that she cared.

The doctor eventually gave my Mom a few days to live. I prayed and prayed. I reread the Scriptures about God being a healer. I had strong faith in God's ability to heal my mother. But after seven days of being in the hospital, my Mom passed. I was so disappointed in God. I was hurt. That was probably the most hurt feeling that I'd ever had in my life. Because of that, I became angry with God. I was mad at Him. I was so upset because I didn't understand why He didn't answer my prayer. My Mom was someone who dedicated herself

PSALM 103:10-14

He has not dealt with us according to our sins, nor punished us according to our iniquities. For as the heavens are high above the earth, great is His mercy toward those who fear Him; as far as the east is from the west, so far has He removed our transgressions from us. As a father pities his children, So the Lord pities those who fear Him. For He knows our frame; He remembers that we are dust.

MATTHEW 18:21-22

Then Peter came to Him and said, "Lord, how often shall my brother sin against me, and I forgive him? Up to seven times?" Jesus said to him, "I do not say to you, up to seven times, but up to seventy times seven."

LUKE 6:37

Judge not, and you shall not be judged. Condemn not, and you shall not be condemned. Forgive, and you will be forgiven.

to the church. She dedicated herself to God. Why did someone who was so good have to die?

I was taught that if you prayed honestly, God would hear you and He would answer your prayer. When God didn't answer my prayer, I thought He had abandoned me. So, as a child, I started doing bad things to spite God. In 8th and 9th grade, I started acting out, and by the time I was in 10th grade, I had moved out of my Dad's house. I got worse and worse, and I didn't know how to handle it. At that time, my family was of very humble means, and we couldn't afford to send me to therapy. I believed there was nowhere I could turn for help, and my life started spiraling out of control. When people looked at me back then, all they saw was a bad little boy. But really, I was just angry with God.

My Dad never gave up on me. He kept reaching out to help me. He tried to get me to go to church, but I didn't want to go. After all, when I had prayed to God for something as important as my Mom's life, God didn't answer my prayer. I just didn't understand the purpose of going to church. The truth, however, was that I was just a child, and I didn't yet understand God's ways.

Nobody understood what I was going through, and I didn't know how to explain it. I wanted to do everything wrong, to break every rule, because doing everything right didn't make sense to me. I felt like my Mom had done everything right, and she didn't get what I thought she deserved.

Now, I know that many people die of cancer every year. Still, I felt like my Mom deserved God's mercy. After all, she was a believer, and she was faithful to God. It was so hurtful to me when God didn't answer my prayer on her behalf. I didn't want to be obedient to God or to my father anymore. I knew God was a healer because I had been reading the Bible my entire life. And I knew that God had healed cancer before. I knew that it wasn't impossible for God to heal my Mom. I had seen God do the impossible all throughout Scripture. He had parted the Red Sea. He had given sight to the blind and healed the sick. So why couldn't He heal my Mom?

I spiralled out of control for more than 20 years.

The Prodigal Son

In 1995, the Feds came to my house on drug conspiracy charges. The head investigator said to the other officers, "How did we miss that Winston had a house phone in here that we could have tapped?" They didn't find the house phone because God saved me. Still, I was disobedient. Satan was in my ear, telling me to stray from God. I was trying to make money my way, instead of making money God's Way.

In 2000, an undercover agent came to my house. Because of his white beard, the people in the community nicknamed him Santa Claus. When he came to my door, something immediately said to me, don't touch him. He's dirty. God saved me again.

A year later, Greensboro police officers pulled me over, along with my friends BoBo, Will, and a few others on I-20 coming from Atlanta. We were in two separate vehicles. They brought dogs and searched our cars for a couple of hours. I couldn't believe even the dogs didn't find anything in those vehicles. We were dirty, and we all should have gone to prison, but God saved us.

EPHESIANS 4:32

And be kind to one another, tenderhearted, forgiving one another, even as God in Christ forgave you.

I know for a fact that God changed my story when I didn't deserve it. He saved me so I could help others. This is why I give God the highest praise, and why I demand that others do things the right way — God's Way.

Now, I know some may say, "Wow, he did wrong and got away with it." Let me tell you that is not true, I didn't go to prison, but I paid a price for more than twenty years. During my times of dealing drugs, I got caught with marijuana possession twice, paid fines, did a few days in jail, had my license suspended, and was on probation. But all of that was a small price to pay compared to what else I had to endure. God punished me, but gracefully. Unfortunately, the police officers in Thomson and Warren County mistakenly recorded the marijuana charges in their system as marijuana felony charges, when both were only misdemeanors. For over ten years, I met with officials to get this resolved and corrected on my criminal background. This was my punishment for my continued disobedience to God and to my father. My criminal activities haunted me for two decades. Due to this being wrongly reported against my criminal background, I couldn't get a job for years. I was forced to stay in business for some sort of income, even when I wanted to quit. There were so many times I wanted to give up on my business, but I couldn't because I knew those felonies would keep me from being hired and getting a good job.

One of the chiefs in Warren County said to me, "I see it's an error, but I can't change it." The investigator said to me, "It's not on me. The clerk of the court has to take care of these changes." I even spoke with the DA, who told me, "I can't change it either. The officer who charged you has to change it." Well, those officers had all either died or retired, so no one could change the charges against me. I was very discouraged, but this was my punishment.

I went over twenty years with two felonies on my criminal background that shouldn't have been there. When I would apply for jobs, they would ask if I had ever been convicted of a felony, and I would check "no" on my application because I hadn't been; it was just an error. I had been blessed to only have misdemeanors. However, when they pulled my criminal background, it looked like I was a liar because it was in the system as felonies. I would get hired on jobs while they waited for my criminal background to come back, and then when the company saw my record, they would let me go. One time after I got fired for my criminal background check, the chief of police wrote a letter on my behalf stating that it was an error, but it still didn't help me. I didn't go to prison, but trust me, I paid a price for over twenty years for selling drugs. I missed dozens of good job opportunities. This situation forced me to study and learn how to have a successful business. Nobody could do anything for me as it related to those felonies, because nobody can override what God does until he's ready to remove it.

> I don't want you to get discouraged when things are not going right in your business — when you ask God for help, but God doesn't provide right away, or He doesn't provide in the way that you have asked. God always does things for a reason, but we don't always know what that reason is. I don't want you to give up on God because you don't get the results you want.

Finally, I started to turn my life around. I wanted to pursue prison ministry so that I could help inmates that had gone down the same wrong path as me. However, without this error being fixed on my criminal background, it wasn't going to happen. I prayed to God, asking Him to intercede for me and release me from this punishment. A few days later, a judge came to my shop to get tires and I told her my story. She told me to come by her office. She said she knew exactly how to fix the error for me in McDuffie County. The McDuffie County judge assisted the Warren County clerk in making the correct changes in their county as well. I later went to get a copy of my criminal record, and it was fixed and deleted.

When God felt He could trust me to make money His Way, then He sent Judge Valerie Burley to my shop. God has always been there for me. Take it from me, God may lighten your punishment, but you will never do wrong and get by.

In 2002, I finally made a vow to God, I would never live that life again. I worked for a few years, then later I started my own business. I wanted to live according to God's words; however, I had many ups and downs in business while living for God, and life was challenging at times. I was in communication with God because I felt like He wasn't showing me the love I felt I deserved. I wanted my business to prosper, and I knew God could make that happen for me. When I wasn't getting those results, I was discouraged, and I once again began to question God. God reminded me of all the times He had saved me. He protected me. Then, He sent me a revelation.

The Prodigal Son Returns

In 2011, I was sitting on my back porch, reading my Bible. God was slowly leading me back to Him.

He wanted me to return to church, but it had to be done in His time, because God's time is always the right time. I was reading Scripture, and I turned to the story about Judas' betrayal of Jesus. Jesus was getting ready to go to the cross, and He prayed to God and said, "Father, let this cup pass from me." He asked God three times, "Let this cup pass from me." I was reading the passage, and I prayed to God, "Lord, please give me an understanding of what I am reading."

God came to me and said, "You see? Jesus asked me three times in prayer, 'Let this cup pass from me.' And I wouldn't even answer the prayers of my own Son. When you prayed to me to heal your Mom from cancer, I heard your prayers, but it was not in My will to heal her on earth."

God healed me the moment that He showed me that He didn't even answer Jesus' prayer. When God gave me that revelation, that released me. Now I realized that I can't be mad at God. That's how He operates. He didn't even give Jesus what He prayed for, and I can't say that my Mom is better than Christ.

My Dad had tried to get me to come to church, and I wouldn't even go. I just thought, what's the use? I never had anyone who could explain to me how to deal with my Mom's death. So, I went twenty-three years because I never had anyone to help me. For twenty-three years, I was trying to break in prison, because I just wanted to be a disobedient, lawbreaking kid. I was hurt and angry, and I didn't want to do what was right.

When my Mom died, my Dad was forty years old and having to take care of five kids, so he never got the time to sit down with me and talk things out. He was processing his own profound grief at my Mom's passing. I was one of the oldest.

LUKE 15:21

And the son said to him, "Father, I have sinned against heaven and in your sight, and am no longer worthy to be called your son."

MATTHEW 6:15

But if you do not forgive men their trespasses, neither will your Father forgive your trespasses.

ACTS 2:38

Then Peter said to them, "Repent, and let every one of you be baptized in the name of Jesus Christ for the remission of sins; and you shall receive the gift of the Holy Spirit.

My dad was left with a three-year-old daughter to take care of. He didn't know how to help me with the kinds of emotional struggles that I was going through because he was suffering as well.

Then as I got older, I wasn't able to talk to anyone about my reasons for being angry at God. I was so ashamed. It was there in the middle of my heart, like this hollow place. I never dealt with it in the right way.

In my view, my Mom did everything right. And then to do everything right and die of cancer, I thought that it was just unfair. To a twelve-year-old child, it seemed like God was taking all her faithfulness and just throwing it away. I saw my Mom fast for three days without eating or drinking. I saw my Mom dedicate her Sabbath to the Lord and nothing else. I saw my Mom go to church five days a week. She would go to early morning services and then come back two or three nights during the week for evening services. I felt like, she of all people should have been spared. I felt like she earned God's mercy. She deserved it. When I didn't get that answer, that destroyed me.

And even though I had turned my back on God, God never turned His back on me.

Through that Scripture, God was showing me that He hadn't forsaken me. Before that day, I had always felt like I hadn't gotten my answer from God. I felt like God hadn't treated my family right. I felt like my Mom didn't get what she deserved. But then God reassured me, "Winston, I wouldn't even answer the prayers of Jesus. I wouldn't even answer the prayers of my own Son. He cried out three times, 'Let this cup pass from me'. There are some prayers that I cannot answer."

God told me that just as it wasn't His will for Jesus to skip the cross, it wasn't His will to keep my

Mom on earth. God told me, "I healed your Mom, but it was on the other side."

I had been doing things that were contrary to the Word of God. It was foolish, but I was angry and discouraged. My relationship with my Mom was really special. It was hurtful to see her in pain. So, when God gave me that scripture, He asked me, "Would you have rather that I had let your Mom stay here, sick and in torment?"

This really showed me that God wanted what was best for her. She is in a place where there is no sickness, no pain, no cancer. She's healed where she is now. We don't want to see our loved ones go. It's so hard to see them walk away from us and go to God. Yet we don't come here to live forever. Our goal is to go and be with the Lord.

From that day forward, my relationship with God changed. That's when I got back into the church, and later into ministry. When God explained that scripture to me, it changed my whole outlook on faith.

In the same way, I don't want you to get discouraged when things are not going right in your business — when you ask God for help, but God doesn't provide right away, or He doesn't provide in the way that you have asked. God always does things for a reason, but we don't always know what that reason is. I don't want you to give up on God because you don't get the results you want. It took me from 1988 to 2011 to come back to the Lord. That's a long time to be away from God. I hoarded that pain for years. I share my pain so that you may learn from it.

When I read that Scripture, it was a sunny day, and I was on my back deck. I've always heard that your parents come back and see you after they pass. When I got done reading the Scripture,

LUKE 22:42

"Father, if it is Your will, take this cup away from Me; nevertheless not My will, but Yours, be done."

EPHESIANS 1:7

In Him we have redemption through His blood, the forgiveness of sins, according to the riches of His grace.

LUKE 15:31-32

And he said to him, "Son, you are always with me, and all that I have is yours. It was right that we should make merry and be glad, for your brother was dead and is alive again, and was lost and is found."

LUKE 23:34

Then said Jesus, "Father, forgive them; for they know not what they do." And they parted His raiment, and cast lots.

I looked up towards Heaven, and I could see my Mom in the sunshine. She was beautiful, as she always was, in a white robe.

And even though I had turned my back on God, God never turned His back on me. All the times that I should have gotten pulled over for drugs and sent to prison — I really believe that God didn't allow that because He knew what I was dealing with. I believe that it was His way of showing me that He always loved me. And He also knew that He needed me to help Him save others from the same path.

> We are all here to serve the Kingdom of God. So, when you are suffering, when you think God has abandoned you, when you beg God to take away the cup He has given you, know that it is all in God's plan. You will succeed. All you have to do is listen to God's word and be obedient to Him.

God knew that I was dealing with all of this, and He knew exactly when to reveal the truth to me. That's why He sent me to that scripture that day. When I read the Scripture, God could begin to explain it to me. I was finally ready.

The Bible says, "For the Word of God is quick and powerful," and God's Word was powerful enough to heal me that day. God explained to me exactly why He healed my Mom in the way that He did. At last, He was confident in me to understand. And in turn, I regained my confidence in Him. Even Christ Himself didn't get the answer He wanted from God. God's will is His own, and we must trust in Him.

From that day forward, I started living the way that I was always taught to live. The way my mother and father raised me. All you have to do is listen to God's Word and shun the devil. We can't understand what God's plan is. But we have to accept that there is a plan in place. Just because we don't understand it doesn't mean that God has abandoned us.

I wanted my Mom here on earth with me. I wanted her in my presence. But those were the wants of a small child. I wanted everything my way. And my way was, "God, please heal her so she can stay with me on earth." But that wasn't His plan. He wanted my Mom in Heaven. He brought her to Him, and He healed her.

That revelation released me from Satan. The devil had been using my anger at God over my mother's passing to keep me separated from God. He used my disappointment in God to his advantage. That's what Satan wants. So long as I'm pulling away from God, Satan is satisfied. He wants me to be out of alignment with God, to stop doing things in accordance with God's plan. He wants to destroy me, because with each of us that he destroys, he can more easily destroy the Kingdom from the inside out.

Sometimes when we pray for something, God gives it to us because that's His plan. But when we pray for it, and God doesn't give it to us, we have to accept that as His plan as well.

Whatever you ask God for has to be in alignment with His will. God doesn't follow our plans; He follows His plans. Jesus couldn't avoid the cross because God's plan was for Jesus to die so that the world could be saved. God doesn't answer when you're not in alignment. He only answers when your prayers are in accordance with His will.

I know how it feels to shoulder hurt, pain, disappointment, and anger at God. And because of what I've been through, I am able to relate to people who have suffered loss. And maybe that is part of God's plan for who I am. Maybe that's part of why He chose to make me angry with Him for all those years, why He made it take so long for me to come back to Him. Maybe it is so that I can relate to people who are angry with God, people who are struggling, and I can bring them back to the ways of the Lord.

Everything God does is for a reason. We can't understand it at one time. We can't see the big picture. But He does it for a purpose. When we don't understand why He does things, it's easy to be angry with Him. This is why so many people don't have a relationship with God. They are upset and hurt because they can't have it their way. They are used to God mostly giving them what they want, so when they pray for something and don't get it, they get upset and pitch a fit. That's what I was doing. I was pitching a fit. And I pitched that fit for twenty-three years.

I kept doing wrong over and over, but God protected me because He wanted to at least have the opportunity to make peace with me. He wanted me to know that He never turned His back on me. He never did anything differently to me than He did to Christ. Ever since then, I've prayed to God for more understanding of Scripture. I've asked Him to give me the wisdom and knowledge so that when I preach, I can explain it to other people in a way that they can understand. I asked Him to give me that gift so that I can share His Word everywhere I go. I believe that God has imparted on me the gift of knowledge and wisdom so that I can bring other people back to the ways of the Lord.

I got a letter in the mail recently from a parishioner. I had preached at her church about a month before. She wanted me to know the power and goodness of God that I showed her through my testimony.

"Pastor Grier, I wanted to share with you about how your sermon and your testimony helped me. I am always a believer in prayer and in God's healing power. I was walking with a cane since 2014 when I first got sick with vertigo. After your sermon that Sunday in Springfield, I asked God for the impossible, as you told us to do. And I did it with prayer, and believing that God was going to answer my prayer. I want you to know that I have put my cane down, and with my belief and trust in God, I am now walking without my cane. Keep me in prayer that God will continue to heal my body and that I will continue to stay close to God. Thank you so much for letting God use you to share your testimony to help others."

God reminds me every day, "I spared you." At that moment I realized I've never been more loved in my life. God has always been by my side. I used to run the streets. I rebelled against God and my father. I walked around with a pocket full of drugs that I would sell to make money. But for the grace of God, I would have wound up in Federal Prison. God spared me so that I could help Him save others.

I saw many businesses close down during the recession and rough economy in 2008, but God saved mine. I saw people close their businesses during the pandemic in 2019, but God saved mine. God said to me, "Pastor, I loved you even when you were rebellious and disobedient to my words. Never allow Satan to make you think you're in business alone. When you started living righteous and obedient, Satan tried to get you to doubt

Me, but I was always there to protect you. I will not fail you. Your business will prosper so long as you do things My Way."

God gives second chances. Even if you feel that your past failures may not be forgiven, I want to remind you that regardless of what you may have done, God still loves you, and His grace is sufficient. God doesn't take pleasure in our failure; it is His desire that we prosper.

I share my story with you in case you are struggling. In case you feel angry or disappointed with God. God has a will that is unknowable to us. His will was unknowable even to His own Son. And yet God is always working in our behalf. He is always working to build up Kingdom people. He wants us to thrive. He wants us to be successful. He wants our businesses to make money, and He wants us to flourish.

If Christ had not died on the cross, He would not have saved the world. It was painful for Christ to go through the crucifixion. He suffered. But because of His suffering, we are all here as Christians. We are all here to serve the Kingdom of God. So, when you are suffering, when you think God has abandoned you, when you beg God to take away the cup He has given you, know that it is all in God's plan. You will succeed. All you have to do is listen to God's word and be obedient to Him.

Everything God does is for a reason. We can't understand it at one time. We can't see the big picture. But He does it for a purpose.

I had faults, and I've failed. I was just like the Prodigal Son. I was raised by a great father and mother and was taught to make Godly decisions, but I left and decided to go my own way. My father never gave up on me. He would lay hands on me and pray for me that God would deliver me from the hands of the enemy. My Dad was always interceding in prayer for me. He was just like the father of the Prodigal Son; He was waiting for me to come back to God, and finally I did. When I started doing things God's Way, it wasn't easy, but God has always covered my business. I'm not a billionaire, but I'm at peace because I'm making money God's Way, and I'm living for God. Now my Dad, Apostle Winston Grier Sr, my Mom, the late First Lady Betty Grier, and my stepmother are pleased with my life, and that is thanks to the power of my Father in Heaven. All the glory goes to God.

Pastor Grier's Forgiveness Prayer for Your Business

Dear kind and heavenly Father, thank You for Your love and kindness. Thank You for Your grace and mercy. Thank You for protecting my business, and more importantly thank You for staying by me and not giving up on me when I've done wrong. Lord, I will continue to keep my faith in You, even when I'm in a difficult season. God, my hope is in Your relentless power. When man says "no," You're always there with a "yes." When I lose money, when I have bad credit, and when I make poor decisions, You step in and restore me to my proper place in You. God, I thank You for never leaving me alone. I praise You for what You have already accomplished, and I thank You in advance for all the blessings You will bring in the future. Lord, I am still standing on Your promises and waiting for many more things to come to pass. My confidence is in You. Lord, You are worthy of all the honor and the praise. I will bless Your name at all times, and Your praises shall continually be in my mouth. All these blessings I ask for in Your son Jesus' name.

Amen.

Pastor Grier's Offers for You and Your Business

To learn more about these offers, visit:
www.WealthAndKingdom.com

Business Coaching Programs

We offer individual and group coaching programs. Each group has a maximum of twelve disciples, so that everyone receives help that is tailored to their needs. Our team will share what they know from scripture, college, and business experience. Pastor Grier is concerned that so many in the Kingdom lack knowledge about being a business owner, robbing them of their financial inheritance, especially when 3 John 2:1 says, "Beloved, I want more than anything to see you prosper, even as your soul prospers." We have so many that can pray a good prayer, speak in tongues, and quote scriptures, and yet they are financially unstable or flat out broke. In the Bible, Abraham, Solomon, David, Job, and so many scholars of the scriptures prospered financially in business while living out their Kingdom responsibilities — so why aren't we? Our goal is to help business owners and entrepreneurs apply Kingdom principles in business to increase faith and finances. Whether you want to start a business or grow your business, this coaching program will help you. Our team will put together a unique plan for each entrepreneur or business owner. We realize that one size doesn't fit all, and each case will be different, so you can rest assured that your program plan will benefit your bottom line.

Wealth and Kingdom Workshops

Pastor Grier offers seminars designed for your Bible Study, Financial Workshop, or Business Workshop. It is our birthright as Kingdom people to get everything God has for us, and Pastor

Grier will equip you, your congregation, staff, and members to walk in Divine favor. These Workshops are good for churches, faith-based organizations, clubs, etc. Pastor Grier will teach you about financial bondage, breaking generational curses, money management, trusting God for the impossible, relentless faith over loans, and so much more.

Personal Financial Coaching

This is an individual private coaching program designed to help you put together a spending plan, improve your credit, prepare to purchase an automobile or home, plan for retirement, pay your tithes, optimize your taxes, etc. We will find out where your treasure is going, so that we may see what is causing financial strain. We believe scriptures, "For where your treasure is, there your heart will be also" (Matthew 6:21). We want to help you grow financially and spiritually. Pastor Grier is a certified Christian Financial Coach from Light University, and through his years of wisdom and study, he will help you gain peace and financial freedom.

Motivational Speaker

Pastor Grier is a Christian motivational speaker and Christian book author. Pastor Grier enjoys sharing God's Word on the streets, at concerts, and at events. The Pastor strongly believes God's Way is the foundation for building a blessed life. If God is not the foundation, the building will fall. If your audience is looking to be spiritually fed, motivated, and encouraged, Pastor Grier is gifted to do just that. He will teach your audience how to live according to God's Way and grow in their faith and finances.

"I have been an ordained Pastor since 2016. My calling and purpose on earth are to help you increase your faith and your inheritance from God, so that you may unlock Kingdom blessings for your personal life and business."

About Pastor Winston Grier

Pastor Winston Grier has dedicated his life to motivating people both young and old through the teachings of Christ. Pastor Grier was raised as a PK (preacher's kid) — he was taught by his father, Apostle Grier, to make Godly decisions. Unfortunately, Pastor Grier was hard-headed as a young man, and he rebelled against his father's teachings. He left his father's house, but years later, the Lord's grace and mercy brought him back to God.

In 2012, Pastor Grier became a youth minister, and he is now the Pastor of The Church of the Living God in Thomson & Greensboro, GA. He is also the radio host for a Christian radio show, "Changing Our World," on 104.9 FM.

Pastor Grier is certified as a Christian Financial Coach by Light University. He holds an Honorary Doctorate Degree in Christian Counseling from Kingdom Ambassadors Global Institute (KAGI).

As a youth mentor, he truly believes that God has ordained him to help young men grow up to become good men, fathers, and providers. Pastor Grier uses his life experience, his business expertise, and the wisdom he has gained from God to change the lives of teens and young adults.

God has called Pastor Grier to become a Kingdom Leader, and he is now a Christian motivational speaker and business coach. He is the author of *Making Money God's Way*, a guide to building a Kingdom business

Pastor Grier's message is this: "The spirit of the Lord is upon me. God has called me to distribute encouraging words to those with heavy hearts, preach good news to the poor, enlighten the eyes of the blind, and release God's people from spiritual and financial bondage."

www.ingramcontent.com/pod-product-compliance
Lightning Source LLC
Chambersburg PA
CBHW071331210326
41597CB00015B/1409